9th Workshop on Natural Language Processing for Computer Assisted Language Learning (NLP4CALL 2020)

AA007951

Gothenburg, Sweden
25 November 2020

Editors:

David Alfter
Elena Volodina
Ildikó Pilán
Herbert Lange
Lars Borin

ISBN: 978-1-7138-2834-1

Printed from e-media with permission by:

Curran Associates, Inc.
57 Morehouse Lane
Red Hook, NY 12571

Some format issues inherent in the e-media version may also appear in this print version.

Copyright© (2020) by the Association for Computational Linguistics
All rights reserved.

Printed with permission by Curran Associates, Inc. (2021)

For permission requests, please contact the Association for Computational Linguistics
at the address below.

Association for Computational Linguistics
209 N. Eighth Street
Stroudsburg, Pennsylvania 18360

Phone: 1-570-476-8006
Fax: 1-570-476-0860

acl@aclweb.org

Additional copies of this publication are available from:

Curran Associates, Inc.
57 Morehouse Lane
Red Hook, NY 12571 USA
Phone: 845-758-0400
Fax: 845-758-2633
Email: curran@proceedings.com
Web: www.proceedings.com

Proceedings of the 9th Workshop on

Natural Language Processing for Computer Assisted Language Learning

(NLP4CALL 2020)

Linköping Electronic Conference Proceedings 175

Photo by Pasi Mämmelä (mammela) Licensed under a Pixabay license:
https://pixabay.com/service/license/

Proceedings of the

9th Workshop on Natural Language Processing for Computer Assisted Language Learning (NLP4CALL 2020)

edited by

David Alfter, Elena Volodina, Ildikó Pilán, Herbert Lange and Lars Borin

Linköping Electronic Conference Proceedings 175
2020

Preface

The workshop series on Natural Language Processing (NLP) for Computer-Assisted Language Learning (NLP4CALL) is a meeting place for researchers working on the integration of Natural Language Processing and Speech Technologies in CALL systems and exploring the theoretical and methodological issues arising in this connection. The latter includes, among others, the integration of insights from Second Language Acquisition (SLA) research, and the promotion of "Computational SLA" through setting up Second Language research infrastructures.

The intersection of Natural Language Processing (or Language Technology / Computational Linguistics) and Speech Technology with Computer-Assisted Language Learning (CALL) brings "understanding" of language to CALL tools, thus making CALL intelligent. This fact has given the name for this area of research – Intelligent CALL, or for short, ICALL. As the definition suggests, apart from having excellent knowledge of Natural Language Processing and/or Speech Technology, ICALL researchers need good insights into second language acquisition theories and practices, as well as knowledge of second language pedagogy and didactics. This workshop therefore invites a wide range of ICALL-relevant research, including studies where NLP-enriched tools are used for testing SLA and pedagogical theories, and vice versa, where SLA theories, pedagogical practices or empirical data and modelled in ICALL tools. The NLP4CALL workshop series is aimed at bringing together competences from these areas for sharing experiences and brainstorming around the future of the field.

We invited submissions:

- that describe research directly aimed at ICALL
- that demonstrate actual or discuss the potential use of existing Language and Speech Technologies or resources for language learning
- that describe the ongoing development of resources and tools with potential usage in ICALL, either directly in interactive applications, or indirectly in materials, application, or curriculum development, e.g. learning material generation, assessment of learner texts and responses, individualized learning solutions, provision of feedback
- that discuss challenges and/or research agenda for ICALL
- that describe empirical studies on language learner data

This year a special focus was given to work done on second language vocabulary and grammar profiling, as well as the use of crowdsourcing for creating, collecting, and curating data in NLP projects. We encouraged paper presentations and software demonstrations describing the above-mentioned themes primarily, but not exclusively, for the Nordic languages.

A new feature in this year's workshop is the special *research notes* session. This session included short talks about ongoing unfinished research that collaborating teams were eager to discuss with the community and get feedback. We tested this feature for the first time with an intention to evaluate its impact and utility for future uses. This time around, we did not circulate a separate call for papers/abstracts but selected for inclusion in the session the papers that were rejected but had at least one positive review. Additionally, we invited two moderators, **Torsten Zesch** and **Johannes Graën**, each of whom was also given the possibility to present ongoing research.

This year, we had the pleasure to welcome two invited speakers: Mark Brenchley (Cambridge Assessment English) and Magali Paquot (Université catholique de Louvain).

Dr **Mark Brenchley** is Senior Research Manager at Cambridge Assessment English. Mark manages research supporting the development and validation of Cambridge English products in the areas of speaking and writing, as well as vocabulary and grammar more broadly. He specialises in the application of corpus-based methodologies and is responsible for maintaining and developing the

David Alfter, Elena Volodina, Ildikó Pilán, Herbert Lange and Lars Borin 2020. Preface. *Proceedings of the 9th Workshop on Natural Language Processing for Computer Assisted Language Learning (NLP4CALL 2020).* Linköping Electronic Conference Proceedings 175: i–iv.

company's internal corpus architecture, including the Cambridge Learner Corpus. His current work, in particular, focuses on the development and validation of auto-marking technologies.

In his talk, *What is an NLP NLP? Considerations from an L2 Assessment Perspective,* he offered a more philosophical perspective on the role of NLP in second language assessment, focusing on the question of what it might actually mean for something to be an "NLP NLP"; that is, a natural language processed, natural language profile. In general, he explored the relationship between NLP and L2 profiles with regard to the wider notion of validity as a key assessment concept.

Dr **Magali Paquot** is an FNRS research associate at the Centre for English Corpus Linguistics, UCLouvain. She specializes in the use of learner corpora to study key topics in SLA and is particularly interested in methodological issues. She is co-editor in chief of the International Journal of Learner Corpus Research and one of the founding members of the Learner Corpus Research Association.

In her talk, *Crowdsourcing as a means to democratize access to L2 enriched data: the case of L2 proficiency*, she reported on the first results of the Crowdsourcing Language Assessment Project (CLAP), which aims to investigate whether crowdsourcing can offer practical solutions to the time and cost difficulties often associated with foreign language proficiency assessment. More specifically, CLAP explores whether and how a crowd of people can be used to assess learner texts reliably and validly.

Previous workshops

This workshop follows a series of workshops on NLP4CALL organized by the NEALT Special Interest Group on Intelligent Computer-Assisted Language Learning (SIG-ICALL[1]). The workshop series has previously been financed by the Center for Language Technology at the University of Gothenburg, the SweLL project[2], and the Swedish Research Council's conference grant. Currently the funding comes from Språkbanken Text[3] and the L2 profiling project[4].

Submissions to the nine workshop editions have targeted a wide range of languages, ranging from well-resourced languages (Chinese, German, English, French, Portuguese, Russian, Spanish) to lesser-resourced languages (Erzya, Arabic, Estonian, Irish, Komi-Zyrian, Meadow Mari, Saami, Udmurt, Võro). Among these, several Nordic languages have been targeted, namely Danish, Estonian, Finnish, Icelandic, Norwegian, Saami, Swedish and Võro. The wide scope of the workshop is also evident in the affiliations of the participating authors as illustrated in Table 1.

Country	2012-2020 (# speaker/co-author affiliations)
Algeria	1
Australia	2
Belgium	5
Canada	4
Denmark	3
Egypt	1
Estonia	3
Finland	9
France	9

[1] https://spraakbanken.gu.se/en/research/themes/icall/sig-icall

[2] https://spraakbanken.gu.se/en/projects/swell

[3] https://spraakbanken.gu.se

[4] https://spraakbanken.gu.se/en/projects/l2profiles

Germany	79
Iceland	4
Ireland	2
Japan	2
Lithuania	1
Netherlands	2
Norway	13
Portugal	5
Russia	10
Slovakia	1
Spain	3
Sweden	64
Switzerland	10
UK	2
US	7

Table 1. NLP4CALL speakers' and co-authors' affiliations, 2012-2020

The acceptance rate has varied between 50% and 77%, the average being 65% (see Table 2).

Although the acceptance rate is rather high, the reviewing process has always been very rigorous with two to three double-blind reviews per submission. This indicates that submissions to the workshop have usually been of high quality.

Workshop year	**Submitted**	**Accepted**	**Acceptance rate**
2012	12	8	67%
2013	8	4	50%
2014	13	10	77%
2015	9	6	67%
2016	14	10	72%
2017	13	7	54%
2018	16	11	69%
2019	16	10	63%
2020	7	4	57%

Table 2: Submissions and acceptance rates, 2012-2020

We would like to thank our Program Committee for providing detailed feedback for the reviewed papers:

- Lars Ahrenberg, Linköping University, Sweden
- David Alfter, University of Gothenburg, Sweden
- Claudia Borg, University of Malta, Malta
- António Branco, Universidade de Lisboa, Portugal
- Mark Brenchley, Cambridge Assessment English, UK
- Jill Burstein, Educational Testing Service, US
- Andrew Caines, University of Cambridge, UK
- Xiaobin Chen, Universität Tübingen, Germany
- Kordula de Kuthy, Universität Tübingen, Germany
- Simon Dobnik, University of Gothenburg, Sweden
- Thomas François, Université catholique de Louvain, Belgium
- Johannes Graën, University of Gothenburg, Sweden and Universitat Pompeu Fabra, Spain
- Andrea Horbach, University of Duisburg-Essen, Germany
- Herbert Lange, University of Gothenburg, Sweden and Chalmers Institute of Technology, Sweden

- Peter Ljunglöf, University of Gothenburg, Sweden and Chalmers Institute of Technology, Sweden
- Verena Lyding, EURAC research, Italy
- Beata Megyesi, Uppsala University, Sweden
- Detmar Meurers, Universität Tübingen, Germany
- Margot Mieskes, University of Applied Sciences Darmstadt, Germany
- Lionel Nicolas, EURAC research, Italy
- Ulrike Pado, Hochschule für Technik Stuttgart, Germany
- Magali Paquot, Université catholique de Louvain, Belgium
- Ildikó Pilán, Norwegian Computing Center, Norway
- Robert Reynolds, Brigham Young University, US
- Gerold Schneider, University of Zurich, Switzerland
- Egon Stemle, EURAC research, Italy
- Anaïs Tack, Université catholique de Louvain, Belgium and KU Leuven, Belgium
- Irina Temnikova, Mitra Translations, Bulgaria
- Francis M. Tyers, Indiana University Bloomington, US and Higher School of Economics Moscow, Russia
- Sowmya Vajjala, National Research Council, Canada
- Elena Volodina, University of Gothenburg, Sweden
- Zarah Weiss, Universität Tübingen, Germany
- Mats Wirén, Stockholm University, Sweden
- Torsten Zesch, University of Duisburg-Essen, Germany
- Ramon Ziai, Universität Tübingen, Germany
- Robert Östling, Stockholm University, Sweden

We intend to continue this workshop series, which so far has been the only ICALL-relevant recurring event based in the Nordic countries. Our intention is to co-locate the workshop series with the two major LT events in Scandinavia, SLTC (the Swedish Language Technology Conference) and NoDaLiDa (Nordic Conference on Computational Linguistics), thus making this workshop an annual event. Through this workshop, we intend to profile ICALL research in Nordic countries as well as beyond, and we aim at providing a dissemination venue for researchers active in this area.

Workshop website:

https://spraakbanken.gu.se/en/research/themes/icall/nlp4call-workshop-series/nlp4call2020

Workshop organizers

David Alfter[1], Elena Volodina[1], Ildikó Pilán[2], Herbert Lange[3], Lars Borin[1]

[1] Språkbanken, University of Gothenburg, Sweden

[2] Norwegian Computing Center, Norway

[3] University of Gothenburg, Sweden and Chalmers Institute of Technology, Sweden

Acknowledgements

We gratefully acknowledge the financial support from *Språkbanken Text* and the *L2 profiles for Swedish* project.

Contents

Substituto – A Synchronous Educational Language Game for Simultaneous Teaching and Crowdsourcing

Marianne Grace Araneta
University of Trento

Gülşen Eryiğit
AI & Data Engineering Dep.
Istanbul Technical University

Alexander König
CLARIN ERIC

Ji-Ung Lee
UKP Lab
Technical University of Darmstadt

Ana R. Luís
University of Coimbra
CELGA/ILTEC

Verena Lyding
Institute for Applied Linguistics
Eurac Research Bolzano/Bozen

Lionel Nicolas
Institute for Applied Linguistics
Eurac Research Bolzano/Bozen

Christos Rodosthenous
Open University of Cyprus

Federico Sangati
University of Naples, Italy
OIST University, Japan

Abstract

This paper investigates a general framework for synchronous educational language games that simultaneously allows researchers to crowdsource learner answers in a controlled environment. Our prototype Substituto[1] allows teachers and students to interact in real-time while undergoing language learning exercises; ensuring that the learner's progress is not hurt by the introduction of crowdsourcing elements. We evaluate Substituto with a small-scale user study that focuses on training the use of English verb-particle constructions (VPCs), such as *break down* or *take over*, and test their use with second language learners of English of different proficiency levels over five pilot sessions. With the study we aim to ensure that our prototypical implementation behaves as expected and to identify any major design flaws that should be addressed. The preliminary results we achieved in order to evaluate the educational value, the user experience and the crowdsourcing capacity of Substituto confirm that it has the potential to become a valuable asset for language learning, a pleasant learning instrument and a crowdsourcing tool for collecting linguistic knowledge.

1 Introduction

In the last few years there has been a substantial growth in the number of language learning educational tools, and recent works have shown the importance of gamification and more specifically how game-based student response systems (SRS) help foster student motivation, engagement and learning (Turan and Meral, 2018; Göksün and Gürsoy, 2019). The main problem behind such systems is that teachers – usually with only little control over such tools – no longer play a central part in the educational process, and consequently, are not able to provide students with appropriate feedback and assist them in their progress. On the other hand, handing the teachers complete control over learning tools may place too much burden on them in constructing learning materials and would essentially resolve into a traditional, no-technology approach to education.

With Substituto as our prototype, we present an innovative language game framework that strikes a balance between these two challenges of game-based learning. Driven by well-established NLP technologies it addresses this issue as a game which proposes automatically generated learning content but at the same time involves teachers as moderators and allows them to guide their students through each round. The implemented system enables a teacher to interact in real-time with a group of students either in a virtual setting or a physical classroom scenario.

From an NLP perspective, engaging in the development of educational applications is not restricted to providing tools to real-life use cases, as illustrated by Litman (2016) and Settles et al. (2018). It is also an opportunity to collect students' and teachers' input, which can be used to construct robust NLP resources (e.g., annotated corpora) and educational datasets. While this is a long-term objective of this work, its success is strongly determined by demonstrating its value to education and foster adoption by users. Accordingly, the aim of

This work is licensed under a Creative Commons Attribution 4.0 International Licence. Licence details: http://creativecommons.org/licenses/by/4.0/.

[1]Code, data, and survey form are available at `https://gitlab.com/substituto/nlp4call2020`
All our study participants gave their consent.

Marianne Grace Araneta, Gülşen Eryiğit, Alexander König, Ji-Ung Lee, Ana Luís, Verena Lyding, Lionel Nicolas, Christos Rodosthenous and Federico Sangati 2020. Substituto – A synchronous educational language game for simultaneous teaching and crowdsourcing. *Proceedings of the 9th Workshop on Natural Language Processing for Computer Assisted Language Learning (NLP4CALL 2020).* Linköping Electronic Conference Proceedings 175: 1–9.

the preliminary evaluation was to test the game and confirm its educational value and user experience while observing its potential for crowdsourcing in real-world language learning settings.

In this work, we focus on a single type of exercises for learning English verb-particle constructions (VPCs) in context (such as *give in*, *check out* and *come along*). Students are presented with sentences containing one VPC for which they have to simultaneously find an appropriate synonym (e.g., one or multiple words expressing an identical meaning that is also syntactically appropriate within the context). After submitting their answer, students are shown all the responses given in class and are asked to choose one they approve of (excluding their own response).[2] The teacher then validates the responses by highlighting all the correct answers and points are awarded to students whose answers or votes match the teacher's choice.

The paper is structured as follows. After discussing related work in section 2, we describe the language learning exercise as well as our selection process in section 3. In section 4, we provide details about the application itself. Section 5 introduces the setup of our investigative experiments – carried out in real classroom settings – and provides analysis from a teacher's, data practitioner's, and user's perspective. Our paper concludes in section 6 with a discussion of open challenges and potential future use cases of Substituto.

2 Related Work

Recent years have witnessed a noticeable increase in the use of student response systems (SRS) which allow instructors to pose questions and gather students' responses during a lecture automatically. Studies investigating SRS reported enhanced student engagement (Wang et al., 2008; Mula and Kavanagh, 2009; Patterson et al., 2010; Wang, 2015; Licorish et al., 2017). It has been also shown by Turan and Meral (2018) and Göksün and Gürsoy (2019) that game-based SRS increase the achievement and engagement and decrease the test anxiety levels when compared to non-game-based SRS. It is worth pointing out that SRS in the literature are mostly click-based systems. This makes the investigation of SRS with open answers or no predefined correct answer a new area to explore in teaching. Truong (2016) reviews 51 studies related to adaptive e-learning systems with regard to learning styles and concludes that educational games are still at their early stages.

Gamification in learning games is an important and promising phenomenon (Sangati et al., 2015; Lafourcade et al., 2015). Creative approaches are especially welcome for language learning applications to trigger different learning styles.

Siyanova-Chanturia (2017) discusses the teaching and learning of MWEs as L2. Boers et al. (2017) examined the impact of textual enhancement (i.e., drawing the learner's attention to MWEs by physically manipulating certain aspects of the text to make them easily noticed) on the acquisition of MWEs for L2 learners and showed its positive impact. VPCs are a subtype of multiword expressions (MWEs) which pose interesting challenges for NLP, linguistics and language learning (Hernández, 2019).

Lastly, approaches that combine language learning and crowdsourcing have recently received increasing attention (Lyding et al., 2018; Agerri et al., 2018; Chinkina et al., 2020). For example, Rodosthenous et al. (2019), Lyding et al. (2019) and Rodosthenous et al. (2020), describe a vocabulary trainer with automatically generated content from a semantic network called ConceptNet (Speer et al., 2017) that crowdsources the answers to improve ConceptNet. Substituto partially follows the implicit crowdsourcing paradigm described by Nicolas et al. (2020) to improve NLP datasets that serve as a basis for language learning exercises by utilizing the respective learner answers. The difference of Substituto is that it also involves teachers to serve as supervisors in-between automatically generated exercises and students which allows us to crowdsource additional feedback from experts.

3 Exercise Generation

Although our proposed system can be used for any form of text completion or substitution exercise, we restrict our initial setup for demonstration and testing to the specific use-case of VPC replacement in sentences. VPCs, also known as phrasal verbs, are challenging for non-native speakers mainly because of their non-compositional semantics, which largely means that learners must memorize VPCs as holistic units in addition to learning their syntactic, semantic, and pragmatic use in sentence context. Through pedagogical tools like Substituto, students can familiarize themselves with the au-

[2]Currently, only one response can be chosen, even though multiple responses may be valid.

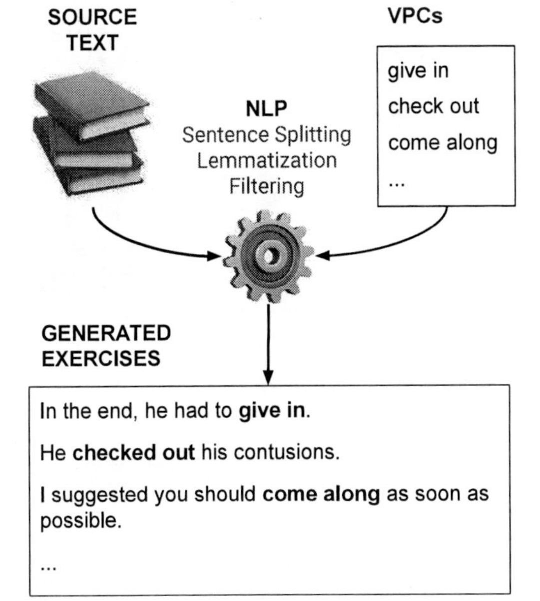

Figure 1: Pre-processing pipeline for exercise sentence selection.

thentic use of this complex language structure in both, receptive and productive vocabulary knowledge.

The goal of the exercises we created is to replace the highlighted VPC with an appropriate synonym which is then evaluated by a teacher. Similar to Boers et al. (2017) we also use textual enhancement for VPCs by bold-facing them. To make our application available to a wide range of users, it is essential to include an automated preprocessing pipeline that allows us to provide good exercise suggestions extracted from various sources (in our case books) to the teachers and allows to scale up the exercise generation at any moment as needed. As a starting point for such an automated procedure to select appropriate sentences for the exercises, we implemented a pre-processing pipeline shown in Figure 1. As our source texts, we selected books from contemporary English literature with Lexile levels of 700 to 1200L and recommendations from Oxford Readers Collections (2015). This reflects B1 difficulty based on the Common European Framework of References for Languages (CEFR). A VPC list of appropriate difficulty is extracted using the English Vocabulary Profile.[3] To extract the sentences which include our target VPCs, we first generate a lemmatized version of a sentence using spaCy (Honnibal and Montani, 2017) for all sentences which do not exceed a maximum number of 25 tokens including punctuation to ensure a good readability on a smartphone. We then filter for sentences which contain a VPC from our predefined list. This allows teachers to select only VPCs which fit their current syllabus to match their classes' proficiency. Afterwards, we apply a set of filter functions to remove sentences which are incomplete or are badly formatted.

Manual Filtering. Although the post-filtering process removes around 40% of the initially extracted sentences, some problematic cases were difficult to address automatically and had to be filtered-out manually (to be addressed in future work). The most relevant encountered issues are:

- Presence of inappropriate or vulgar content.
- Presence of words that require higher-level language proficiency.
- Insufficient context to disambiguate the VPC.
- The sentence contains a word sequence which is homographic to a VPC but it is not a VPC. [4]

For our preliminary study, the participating teachers hand-picked 15 sentences with 15 corresponding VPCs (3 exercise sets of 5 sentences each) that would fit well into their students' curriculum.[5]

4 System Description

The idea behind Substituto is inspired by an existing, turn-based game called PLAGIO[6] where players take turns in choosing the beginning of a sentence from a book and the others complete it. Next, all collected completions (including the original) are displayed and participants try to guess the original continuation. Each player will gain a point if they correctly guessed the original completion, otherwise they will give the point to the player who wrote that completion. PLAGIO finally distributes points for correct guesses of the original sentence and substitutions voted by others. Players earn points by guessing the original sentence and each vote for their provided substitution.

[3] `https://www.englishprofile.org`

[4] For instance: *"What I see under the microscopes are cells sluggishly trying to reconstruct breaks in their walls"* with the underlined word being a noun.

[5] The complete list of VPCs is: break down, break in, break up, check out, come along, come out, end up, fall down, fall over, get in, get on, get out, give in, go away, go down.

[6] `https://www.studiogiochi.com/en/publications/plagio-en-2`

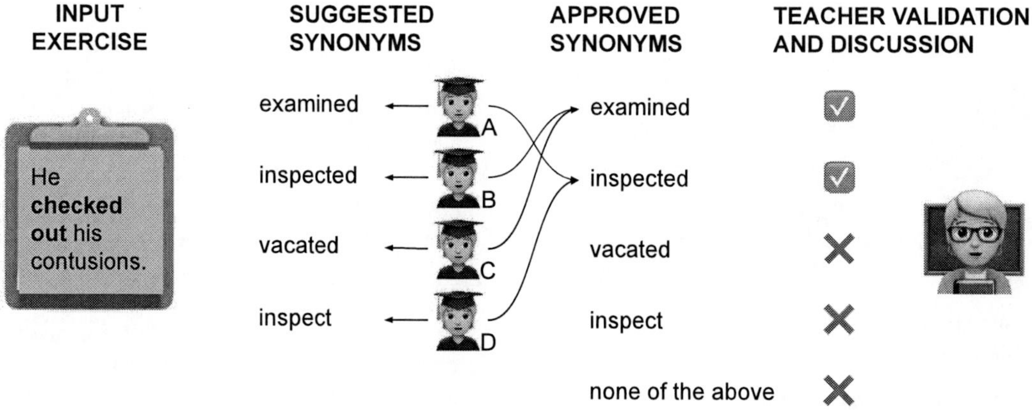

Figure 2: The four phases of each round of Substituto. Here, student A and B receive three points each (for their correct synonym and correct vote), while student C and D receive one point each (for their correct vote).

The interactive game has been implemented as a ChatBot using the Telegram Bot API.[7] This enabled us to speed up development by focusing primarily on the game logic while using the built-in interface available in the messaging application, with keyboard buttons and commands.

Before starting a game, both the teacher and the students have to login to Telegram and search for the bot.[8] Then the teacher has to create a game session by choosing a game name and communicate it to the students so that they can access the same session. Finally, the teacher chooses the exercise set to use in the game.

Each game is divided into five rounds (one per VPC in the exercise set) with each round being composed of four phases (cf. Figure 2):

(1) A specific sentence from the exercise set is automatically selected and displayed to all participants, with the VPC in boldface.

(2) Students type in a synonym of the VPC as a replacement in the given context, preserving the meaning.

(3) Students then vote for a synonym suggested by another student or indicate that no other suggested synonym is correct. They cannot approve their own answers and identical answers are displayed only once.

(4) Finally, the teacher validates which answers are correct (possibly none, or more than one).

[7] `https://core.telegram.org/bots/api`

[8] A running demo is provided in `https://gitlab.com/substituto/nlp4call2020`

Students receive points at the end of each round, rewarding both their productive and receptive language skills. They receive two points for suggesting a correct synonym. During voting, one point is awarded for selecting a synonym that has been approved by the teacher. In case no synonym is deemed correct, only voting "None" is awarded one point. All incorrect votes get a penalty point.

Before the next round starts, the game is put on hold; allowing the teacher to interact with the students and discuss the solved exercise. The game provides a built-in */chat* command that enables participants (students and teacher) to communicate with each other in a group chat that is visible for everyone; allowing teachers to openly engage with the students and provide appropriate hints if they notice that their students have difficulties with an exercise. This is particularly relevant when the game is held virtually without using other ways of interaction such as with a parallel virtual conference or a separate group chat.

5 User Study

In order to investigate the viability of Substituto in real-world teaching scenarios and make preliminary evaluations in terms of educational value, crowdsourcing capacity and user experience, we have conducted five pilot test sessions involving a total number of 26 participants (20 unique students), as reported in Table 1. The tests were conducted in a virtual classroom setting using a parallel video conference setup, with each participant using their own device. Figure 3 shows the teacher's perspective of Substituto during one pilot session.

The first pilot test comprised five university stu-

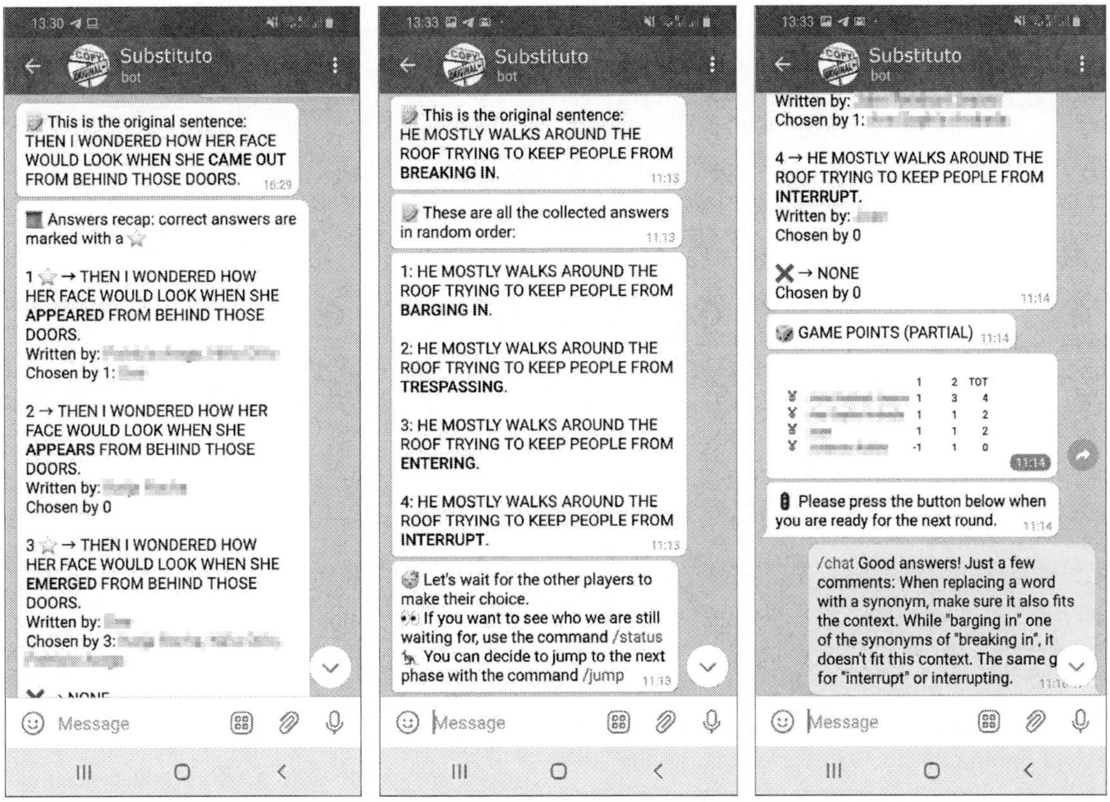

Figure 3: Screenshots from one of our pilot sessions showing the teacher's perspective.

#	L1	CEFR	ppl.	dur. (min)
1	PH	B1-B2	5	44
2	PH	A2-B1	4	29
3	FA, POR, RO	C1	7	30
4	PH	A2-B1	4	25
5	FA, POR	C1	6	60

Table 1: Summary of pilot sessions.

dents whose first language is Filipino but have high English proficiency, ranging from B1 to B2. They completed all rounds of two VPC exercise sets within 40 minutes. The second pilot test was conducted with four Filipino students with A2 to B1 English proficiency and only one exercise set was completed. The third group of students comprised seven students with different L1 backgrounds (Portuguese, Farsi and Romanian) and C1 proficiency. They finished three rounds of one exercise set in 30 minutes. The fourth pilot test was conducted with four Filipino students with varying English proficiency levels, from A2 to B2. The last test comprised six of the seven students in the third pilot test. They completed all five rounds of one exercise set in one hour.

5.1 Educational Analysis

Our preliminary evaluation suggests that Substituto could indeed be useful in a real-world scenario with regards to educational value. We discuss hereafter the teachers' observations in terms of user engagements, quality of student responses, their capacity to evaluate different options and overall learning opportunities. Later in Section 6, we discuss how we intend to further explore the educational value in a quantitative manner.

With respect to user engagement, students were generally engaged during the game and those who were already familiar with each other showed higher levels of engagement – cheering on those who gave good answers or expressing their frustration for not getting a point. There was also much interaction, both between the teacher and students and among students themselves. The teacher would give feedback after each round and students would clarify and discuss the responses. The time spent on feedback and discussion determined the game's pace.

In terms of the quality of student responses,

groups with higher average proficiency, as was the case with the students from the first, third, and fifth session, demonstrated a greater variety of correct answers. In such cases, the teacher-student interaction served the purpose of exploring the sentence context to clarify why some answers may have been more correct than others. For those groups with lower average proficiency, there was less variety and some instances where the literal synonym would be given rather than the contextualized one, as if students had consulted a thesaurus without understanding the word's correct use. For example, given the sentence *"He mostly walks around the roof trying to keep people from **breaking in**"*, with *"breaking in"* as the target VPC, one response was *"barging in"*, while another was *"interrupt"*. While these two are synonyms of *"breaking in"*, they do not fit the context of the sentence. This became an opportunity for the teacher to discuss the importance of context when looking for synonyms.

Regarding the ability of students to evaluate different options, teachers observed that giving students the chance to see correct responses of their fellow students constitutes a valuable learning opportunity that serves to increase their creative use of language. The point system encourages students to give the best possible response but it also triggers discussion among students who feel the need to understand why some answers are better than others. Teachers made use of the chat option to give feedback on student responses; but it was also used to cheer on those who were leading and encourage those who were trailing behind. Being able to trace responses to those who answered them was helpful in monitoring their progress, especially for students who are struggling.

More problematic aspects however have also been identified. With respect to the evaluation of multiple answers, the game allows the selection of more than one correct response, but they all receive the same number of points. This may not reflect "degrees of correctness", where some answers, aside from being correct, reveal a higher level of proficiency that might merit higher points. With respect to the examples, common to all sessions was the difficulty in replacing certain VPCs due to the sentence structure, particularly those VPCs that were followed by a preposition. For example, in the third group, given the sentence: *"All at once the clear voice of Reepicheep **broke in** upon the silence"*, students had difficulty replacing *"broke in"*

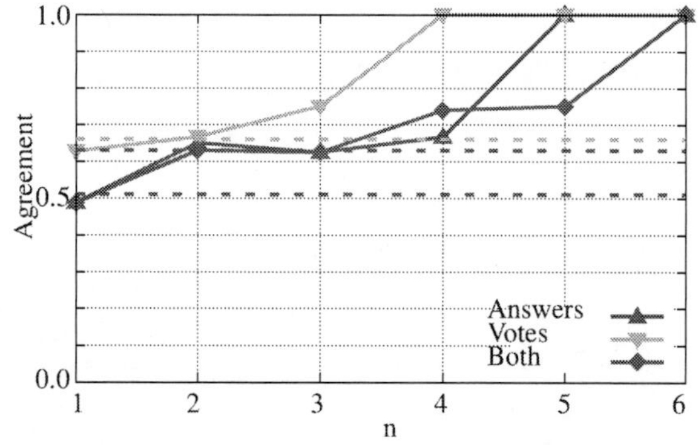

Figure 4: Agreement for different student feedback and thresholds n. Dashed lines show the averaged agreement resulting from a majority vote for each exercise.

with other synonyms due to the prepositional clause *"upon the silence"*, which has a more restricted use. Another observation noted the sentence complexity of the literary sources. Despite the VPCs and reading material being on-level for B1 learners, they were still too challenging for some students.

In terms of learning opportunities, teachers observed during the pilot sessions that the game is more than a vocabulary expansion tool for L2 learners, offering various other learning opportunities. It develops teaching comprehension skills, in so far as students need to fully understand the written examples so as to find an adequate synonym. Because the replacement must both be meaningful and adjusted to the given sentence structure, the game also exercises the students' grammatically correct use of verb forms within context. During the teacher-student discussion time, issues concerning the adequacy of the students' answers (e.g., style, collocation, denotation vs. connotation) were addressed and clarified, promoting language awareness raising opportunities. By and large, the teacher plays a salient role in the learning process, by encouraging class-appropriate discussion and offering real-time and individualized feedback to students.

5.2 Crowdsourcing Analysis

To evaluate the effectiveness of our prototype Substituto in a peer-reviewed learning setup without the teacher's assessment (i.e., an expert opinion), we investigated different levels of student feedback (their answers and votes) to identify correct answers. Our claim is that the collected answers can be used to obtain expert quality labels for a learner-crowdsourced corpus. Due to the restricted exercise context, the students' answers may overlap; resulting in ≈ 0.75 diverse answers per student and exercise. This allowed us to not only consider the number of votes for each answer but also to take into account how often an answer was provided by several students.

We identified correct answers using different thresholds n and computed by how much they agree with the teacher's assessment, e.g., an agreement of 0.66 at $n=2$ votes shows that 66% of the answers which got 2 or more votes were correct.[9] The yellow curve in figure 4 shows that using the students' votes leads to substantially more correct answers than only using the answer quantity (blue) or the sum of answer quantity and vote (red).

We observed a similar outcome when conducting a simple majority vote (tied votes were treated as multiple correct labels) for each exercise as the averaged agreement shows (dashed lines). Collecting the students' votes has an additional advantage; we observed that 73% of the answers with zero votes were also identified as incorrect by the teachers.

Our preliminary results seem to confirm the possibility that collecting more answers and votes, and aggregating them allows us to either build a dataset to provide automatic feedback or to use the aggregated knowledge for upgrading semantic-oriented datasets describing, among other things, synonymy relation between words (e.g., semantic networks such as ConceptNet) or datasets focusing on using synonyms in context (e.g., datasets for automated paraphrasing). We will further discuss the possibility of compiling a gold standard, the required amount of answers to achieve a certain quality, and how to efficiently combine answers of teachers and learners in section 6.

5.3 User Experience Analysis

After concluding the pilot tests all 20 students provided feedback through a structured online survey. The survey addressed (1) the overall experience of using the game, (2) the interaction with the application, and (3) the learning experience. The questionnaire combined multiple-choice answers and open questions. Overall, the evaluation of the students was very positive. 90% of the respondents enjoyed working with Substituto indicating that drawing inspiration from an existing game was a good choice. They particularly liked the gaming aspect and appreciated very much reading the answers of other learners and the feedback provided after each exercise. 75% of the users were positive that the game helped them to improve their verb usage skills. All users confirmed that they were able to follow the instructions and operate the Substituto, while some users commented that the point system was not clear. Also, most respondents appreciated the appearance of the game, and some highlighted positively the scoreboard and status updates.

[9]Note that in our pilot sessions, the maximum possible number of votes is $n = 6$.

6 Conclusion and Future Work

This paper presents Substituto, an online language game that promotes synchronous interaction between teachers and students in a virtual or physical setting while providing the possibility to perform crowdsourcing. The system prototype is in a stable version that supports parallel game sessions and an unlimited number of students for peer-reviewed learning scenarios. We tested the system in five pilot sessions carried out in actual educational environments. Our preliminary study and the results we obtained in terms of educational value, crowdsourcing potential and user experience indicate that Substituto has the potential to become a valuable asset for language learning as a pleasant learning instrument and a crowdsourcing tool that can be used in order to collect linguistic knowledge.

We further plan to address several improvements of Substituto. Whereas we manually selected a set of sentences in our user study, we plan to improve the NLP module for automated sentence retrieval (1) to generate the list of relevant exercises with higher accuracy, and (2) to assess the sentence complexity, which would allow us to tailor exercises to students from a wide range of language proficiency levels. Other mechanisms to control the exercise difficulty include inverting the current task and asking students to find VPC synonyoms for non-VPC words – which we expect to result in more difficult exercises – and including other linguistic resources like ConceptNet (Speer et al., 2017) during generation. In addition, we also foresee to use annotated corpora for the exercise generation, such as for example the PARSEME corpus (Ramisch et al., 2018), which is manually annotated for verbal MWEs. Furthermore, as automated methods cannot fully cover the selection of unsuitable sentences, we will include the possibility for teachers to skip any exercise at the beginning of each round. Following suggestions of teachers from our study, we plan to allow them to distribute bonus points to reward answers that reveal higher proficiency or creativity.

Aside from improving Substituto itself, we intend to conduct more grounded evaluations to confirm our preliminary results. With respect to educational value, a classic strategy would be to work with control groups and compare the improvement of the learning capacity of Substituto against other baselines. Such an approach requires groups of students that are truly comparable to perform evaluations in equivalent conditions, which by themselves are two difficult challenges to tackle. We therefore intend to proceed differently and in a more indirect fashion by involving and formally interviewing a larger number of teachers. By doing so, we intend to obtain an indirect expert evaluation of the educational value.

Regarding the crowdsourcing potential, the involvements of more teachers will allow us to collect a larger amount of learner and teacher answers. We will use the answers of the teachers to create a gold standard that we will manually correct. This gold standard will then be used to evaluate how many aggregated answers from student are needed to decide on the synonymy of two VPCs and will allow us to explore the question of how to best combine the answers of the students and teachers.

Finally, with respect to the user experience, we will take advantage of the larger number of students to run a larger user survey with a new set of questions derived from the practical experience we obtained from this work.

Acknowledgments

We thank all anonymous reviewers for their helpful comments and suggestions. This article is based upon work from COST Action enetCollect (CA16105), supported by COST (European Cooperation in Science and Technology). The work presented in this paper was started during the WG2/WG4/WG5 meeting organized by the Action in November 2019 in Sliema, Malta.

References

Rodrigo Agerri, Montse Maritxalar, Verena Lyding, and Lionel Nicolas. 2018. enetcollect: A new european network for combining language learning with crowdsourcing techniques. *Procesamiento del Lenguaje Natural*, 61:171–174.

Frank Boers, Murielle Demecheleer, Lin He, Julie Deconinck, Hélène Stengers, and June Eyckmans. 2017. Typographic enhancement of multiword units in second language text. *International Journal of Applied Linguistics*, 27(2):448–469.

Maria Chinkina, Simón Ruiz, and Detmar Meurers. 2020. Crowdsourcing evaluation of the quality of automatically generated questions for supporting computer-assisted language teaching. *ReCALL*, 32(2):145–161.

Derya Orhan Göksün and Gülden Gürsoy. 2019. Comparing success and engagement in gamified learning experiences via kahoot and quizizz. *Computers & Education*, 135:15–29.

Simón Eduardo Ruiz Hernández. 2019. *Individual Differences and Instructed Second Language Acquisition: Insights from Intelligent Computer Assisted Language Learning*. Ph.D. thesis, University of Tübingen.

Matthew Honnibal and Ines Montani. 2017. spaCy 2: Natural language understanding with Bloom embeddings, convolutional neural networks and incremental parsing. To appear.

M. Lafourcade, A. Joubert, and N.L. Brun. 2015. *Games with a Purpose (GWAPS)*. Focus Series in Cognitive Science and Knowledge Management. Wiley.

Sherlock Licorish, Jade George, Helen Owen, and Ben Daniel. 2017. "Go Kahoot!" Enriching Classroom Engagement, Motivation and Learning Experience with Games. In *25th International Conference on Computers in Education*, Christchurch, New Zealand.

Diane Litman. 2016. Natural language processing for enhancing teaching and learning. In *Proceedings of the Thirtieth AAAI Conference on Artificial Intelligence*, AAAI'16, pages 4170–4176. AAAI Press.

Verena Lyding, Lionel Nicolas, Branislav Bédi, and Karën Fort. 2018. Introducing the european network for combining language learning and crowdsourcing techniques (enetcollect). *Future-proof CALL: language learning as exploration and encounters–short papers from EUROCALL*, 2018:176.

Verena Lyding, Christos Rodosthenous, Federico Sangati, Umair ul Hassan, Lionel Nicolas, Alexander König, Jolita Horbacauskiene, and Anisia Katinskaia. 2019. v-trel: Vocabulary trainer for tracing word relations-an implicit crowdsourcing approach. In *Proceedings of the International Conference on Recent Advances in Natural Language Processing (RANLP 2019)*, pages 674–683.

Joseph M Mula and Marie Kavanagh. 2009. Click go the students, click-click-click: The efficacy of a student response system for engaging students to improve feedback and performance. *E-Journal of Business Education and Scholarship of Teaching*, 3(1):1–17.

Lionel Nicolas, Verena Lyding, Claudia Borg, Corina Forăscu, Karën Fort, Katerina Zdravkova, Iztok Kosem, Jaka Čibej, Špela Arhar Holdt, Alice Millour, et al. 2020. Creating expert knowledge by relying on language learners: a generic approach for mass-producing language resources by combining implicit crowdsourcing and language learning. In *Proceedings of The 12th Language Resources and Evaluation Conference*, pages 268–278.

Oxford Readers Collections. 2015. *Oxford Readers Collections B1 - B2*. Oxford University Press.

Barbara Patterson, Judith Kilpatrick, and Eric Woebkenberg. 2010. Evidence for teaching practice: The impact of clickers in a large classroom environment. *Nurse education today*, 30(7):603–607.

Carlos Ramisch, Silvio Ricardo Cordeiro, Agata Savary, Veronika Vincze, Verginica Barbu Mititelu, Archna Bhatia, Maja Buljan, Marie Candito, Polona Gantar, Voula Giouli, Tunga Güngör, Abdelati Hawwari, Uxoa Iñurrieta, Jolanta Kovalevskaitė, Simon Krek, Timm Lichte, Chaya Liebeskind, Johanna Monti, Carla Parra Escartín, Behrang QasemiZadeh, Renata Ramisch, Nathan Schneider, Ivelina Stoyanova, Ashwini Vaidya, Abigail Walsh, Cristina Aceta, Itziar Aduriz, Jean-Yves Antoine, Špela Arhar Holdt, Gözde Berk, Agnė Bielinskienė, Goranka Blagus, Loic Boizou, Claire Bonial, Valeria Caruso, Jaka Čibej, Matthieu Constant, Paul Cook, Mona Diab, Tsvetana Dimitrova, Rafael Ehren, Mohamed Elbadrashiny, Hevi Elyovich, Berna Erden, Ainara Estarrona, Aggeliki Fotopoulou, Vassiliki Foufi, Kristina Geeraert, Maarten van Gompel, Itziar Gonzalez, Antton Gurrutxaga, Yaakov Ha-Cohen Kerner, Rehab Ibrahim, Mihaela Ionescu, Kanishka Jain, Ivo-Pavao Jazbec, Teja Kavčič, Natalia Klyueva, Kristina Kocijan, Viktória Kovács, Taja Kuzman, Svetlozara Leseva, Nikola Ljubešić, Ruth Malka, Stella Markantonatou, Héctor Martínez Alonso, Ivana Matas, John McCrae, Helena de Medeiros Caseli, Mihaela Onofrei, Emilia Palka-Binkiewicz, Stella Papadelli, Yannick Parmentier, Antonio Pascucci, Caroline Pasquer, Maria Pia di Buono, Vandana Puri, Annalisa Raffone, Shraddha Ratori, Anna Riccio, Federico Sangati, Vishakha Shukla, Katalin Simkó, Jan Šnajder, Clarissa Somers, Shubham Srivastava, Valentina Stefanova, Shiva Taslimipoor, Natasa Theoxari, Maria Todorova, Ruben Urizar, Aline Villavicencio, and Leonardo Zilio. 2018. Annotated corpora and tools of the PARSEME shared task on automatic identification of verbal multiword expressions (edition 1.1). LINDAT/CLARIAH-CZ digital library at the Institute of Formal and Applied Linguistics (ÚFAL), Faculty of Mathematics and Physics, Charles University.

Christos Rodosthenous, Verena Lyding, Federico Sangati, Alexander König, Umair ul Hassan, Lionel Nicolas, Jolita Horbacauskiene, Anisia Katinskaia, and Lavinia Aparaschivei. 2020. Using crowdsourced exercises for vocabulary training to expand conceptnet. In *Proceedings of The 12th Language Resources and Evaluation Conference*, pages 307–316.

Christos T. Rodosthenous, Verena Lyding, Alexander König, Jolita Horbacauskiene, Anisia Katinskaia, Umair ul Hassan, Nicos Isaak, Federico Sangati, and Lionel Nicolas. 2019. Designing a prototype architecture for crowdsourcing language resources. In *Proceedings of the Poster Session of the 2nd Conference on Language, Data and Knowledge (LDK 2019), Leipzig, Germany, May 21, 2019*, volume 2402 of *CEUR Workshop Proceedings*, pages 17–23. CEUR-WS.org.

Federico Sangati, Stefano Merlo, and Giovanni Moretti. 2015. School-tagging: interactive language exercises in classrooms. In *Language Teaching, Learning and Technology (LTLT-2015)*, pages 16–19, Leipzig, Germany.

Burr Settles, Chris Brust, Erin Gustafson, Masato Hagiwara, and Nitin Madnani. 2018. Second language acquisition modeling. In *Proceedings of the Thirteenth Workshop on Innovative Use of NLP for Building Educational Applications*, pages 56–65, New Orleans, Louisiana. Association for Computational Linguistics.

Anna Siyanova-Chanturia. 2017. Researching the teaching and learning of multi-word expressions. *Language Teaching Research*, 21(3):289–297.

Robyn Speer, Joshua Chin, and Catherine Havasi. 2017. Conceptnet 5.5: An open multilingual graph of general knowledge. In *Proceedings of the Thirty-First AAAI Conference on Artificial Intelligence*, AAAI'17, page 4444–4451. AAAI Press.

Huong May Truong. 2016. Integrating learning styles and adaptive e-learning system: Current developments, problems and opportunities. *Computers in Human Behavior*, 55:1185 – 1193.

Zeynep Turan and Elif Meral. 2018. Game-based versus to non-game-based: The impact of student response systems on students'achievements, engagements and test anxieties. *Informatics in Education*, 17(1):105–116.

A. I. Wang, T. Øfsdahl, and O. K. Mørch-Storstein. 2008. An evaluation of a mobile game concept for lectures. In *2008 21st Conference on Software Engineering Education and Training*, pages 197–204.

Alf Inge Wang. 2015. The wear out effect of a game-based student response system. *Computers & Education*, 82:217–227.

The Teacher-Student Chatroom Corpus

Andrew Caines[1] Helen Yannakoudakis[2] Helena Edmondson[3] Helen Allen[4]
Pascual Pérez-Paredes[5] Bill Byrne[6] Paula Buttery[1]

[1] ALTA Institute & Computer Laboratory, University of Cambridge, U.K.
{andrew.caines|paula.buttery}@cl.cam.ac.uk
[2] Department of Informatics, King's College London, U.K.
helen.yannakoudakis@kcl.ac.uk
[3] Theoretical & Applied Linguistics, University of Cambridge, U.K.
hle24@cantab.ac.uk
[4] Cambridge Assessment, University of Cambridge, U.K.
allen.h@cambridgeenglish.org
[5] Faculty of Education, University of Cambridge, U.K.
pfp23@cam.ac.uk
[6] Department of Engineering, University of Cambridge, U.K.
bill.byrne@eng.cam.ac.uk

Abstract

The Teacher-Student Chatroom Corpus (TSCC) is a collection of written conversations captured during one-to-one lessons between teachers and learners of English. The lessons took place in an online chatroom and therefore involve more interactive, immediate and informal language than might be found in asynchronous exchanges such as email correspondence. The fact that the lessons were one-to-one means that the teacher was able to focus exclusively on the linguistic abilities and errors of the student, and to offer personalised exercises, scaffolding and correction. The TSCC contains more than one hundred lessons between two teachers and eight students, amounting to 13.5K conversational turns and 133K words: it is freely available for research use. We describe the corpus design, data collection procedure and annotations added to the text. We perform some preliminary descriptive analyses of the data and consider possible uses of the TSCC.

1 Introduction & Related Work

We present a new corpus of written conversations from one-to-one, online lessons between English language teachers and learners of English. This is the Teacher-Student Chat Corpus (TSCC) and it is openly available for research use[1]. TSCC currently contains 102 lessons between 2 teachers and 8 students, which in total amounts to 13.5K conversational turns and 133K word tokens, and it will continue to grow if funding allows.

The corpus has been annotated with grammatical error corrections, as well as discourse and teaching-focused labels, and we describe some early insights gained from analysing the lesson transcriptions. We also envisage future use of the corpus to develop dialogue systems for language learning, and to gain a deeper understanding of the teaching and learning process in the acquisition of English as a second language.

We are not aware of any such existing corpus, hence we were motivated to collect one. To the best of our knowledge, the TSCC is the first to feature one-to-one online chatroom conversations between teachers and students in an English language learning context. There are of course many conversation corpora prepared with both close discourse analysis and machine learning in mind. For instance, the Cambridge and Nottingham Corpus of Discourse in English (CANCODE) contains spontaneous conversations recorded in a wide variety of informal settings and has been used to study the grammar of spoken interaction (Carter and McCarthy, 1997). Both versions 1 and 2 of

This work is licensed under a Creative Commons Attribution-NonCommercial-ShareAlike 4.0 International Licence. Licence details: http://creativecommons.org/licenses/by-nc-sa/4.0

[1] Available for download from https://forms.gle/oW5fwTTZfZcTkp8v9

Andrew Caines, Helen Yannakoudakis, Helena Edmondson, Helen Allen, Pascual Pérez-Paredes, Bill Byrne and Paula Buttery 2020. The teacher-student chatroom corpus. *Proceedings of the 9th Workshop on Natural Language Processing for Computer Assisted Language Learning (NLP4CALL 2020).* Linköping Electronic Conference Proceedings 175: 10–9.

the British National Corpus feature transcriptions of spoken conversation captured in settings ranging from parliamentary debates to casual discussion among friends and family (BNC Consortium, 2001; Love et al., 2017).

Corpora based on educational interactions, such as lectures and small group discussion, include the widely-used Michigan Corpus of Academic Spoken English (MICASE) (Simpson et al., 2002), TOEFL 2000 Spoken and Written Academic Language corpus (Biber et al., 2004), and Limerick Belfast Corpus of Academic Spoken English (LIBEL) (O'Keeffe and Walsh, 2012). Corpora like the ones listed so far, collected with demographic and linguistic information about the contributors, enable the study of sociolinguistic and discourse research questions such as the interplay between lexical bundles and discourse functions (Csomay, 2012), the interaction of roles and goal-driven behaviour in academic discourse (Evison, 2013), and knowledge development at different stages of higher education learning (Atwood et al., 2010).

On a larger scale, corpora such as the Multi-Domain Wizard-of-Oz datasets (MultiWOZ) contain thousands of goal-directed dialogue collected through crowdsourcing and intended for the training of automated dialogue systems (Budzianowski et al., 2018; Eric et al., 2020). Other work has involved the collation of pre-existing conversations on the web, for example from Twitter (Ritter et al., 2010), Reddit (Schrading et al., 2015), and movie scripts (Danescu-Niculescu-Mizil and Lee, 2011). Such datasets are useful for training dialogue systems to respond to written inputs – so-called 'chatbots' – which in recent years have greatly improved in terms of presenting some kind of personality, empathy and world knowledge (Roller et al., 2020), where previously there had been relatively little of all three. The improvement in chatbots has caught the attention of, and in turn has been driven by, the technology industry, for they have clear commercial applications in customer service scenarios such as helplines and booking systems.

As well as personality, empathy and world knowledge, if chatbots could also assess the linguistic proficiency of a human interlocutor, give pedagogical feedback, select appropriate tasks and topics for discussion, maintain a long-term memory of student language development, *and* begin and close a lesson on time, that would be a teaching chatbot of sorts. We know that the list above represents a very demanding set of technological challenges, but the first step towards these more ambitious goals is to collect a dataset which allows us to analyse how language teachers operate, how they respond to student needs and structure a lesson. This dataset may indicate how we can begin to address the challenge of implementing a language teaching chatbot.

We therefore set out to collect a corpus of one-to-one teacher-student language lessons in English, since we are unaware of existing corpora of this type. The most similar corpora we know of are the Why2Atlas Human-Human Typed Tutoring Corpus which centred on physics tutoring (Rosé et al., 2003), the chats collected between native speakers and learners of Japanese using a virtual reality university campus (Toyoda and Harrison, 2002), and an instant messaging corpus between native speakers and learners of German (Höhn, 2017). This last corpus was used to design an other-initiated self-repair module in a dialogue system for language learning, the kind of approach which we aim to emulate in this project. In addition there is the CIMA dataset released this year which involves one-to-one written conversation between crowdworkers role-playing as teachers and students (Stasaski et al., 2020), but the fact that they are not genuinely teachers and learners of English taking part in real language lessons means that the data lack authenticity (albeit the corpus is well structured and useful for chatbot development).

2 Corpus design

We set out a design for the TSCC which was intended to be convenient for participants, efficient for data processing, and would allow us to make the data public. The corpus was to be teacher-centric: we wanted to discover how teachers deliver an English language lesson, adapt to the individual student, and offer teaching feedback to help students improve. On the other hand, we wanted as much diversity in the student group as possible, and therefore aimed to retain teachers during the data collection process as far as possible, but to open up student recruitment as widely as possible.

In order to host the lessons, we considered several well-known existing platforms, including Facebook Messenger, WhatsApp, and Telegram, but decided against these due firstly to concerns about connecting people unknown to each other, where the effect of connecting them could be long-lasting and unwanted (*i.e.* ongoing messaging or social networking beyond the scope of the TSCC project). Secondly we had concerns that since those platforms retain user data to greater or lesser extent, we were requiring that study participants give up some personal information to third party tech firms – which they may already be doing, but we didn't want to *require* this of the participants.

We consequently decided to use ephemeral chatrooms to host the lessons, and looked into using existing platforms such as Chatzy, but again had privacy concerns about the platform provider retaining their own copy of the lesson transcriptions (a stated clause in their terms and conditions) for unknown purposes. Thus we were led to developing our own chatroom in Shiny for R (Chang et al., 2020). In designing the chatroom we kept it as minimal and uncluttered as possible; it had little extra functionality but did the basics of text entry, username changes, and link highlighting.

Before recruiting participants, we obtained ethics approval from our institutional review board, on the understanding that lesson transcripts would be anonymised before public release, that participant information forms would be at an appropriate linguistic level for intermediate learners of English, and that there would be a clear procedure for participants to request deletion of their data if they wished to withdraw from the study. Funding was obtained in order to pay teachers for their participation in the study, whereas students were not paid for participation on the grounds that they were receiving a free one-to-one lesson.

3 Data collection

We recruited two experienced, qualified English language teachers to deliver the online lessons one hour at a time, on a one-to-one basis with students. The teacher-student pair were given access to the chatroom web application (Figure 1) and we obtained a transcription of the lesson at the end of the lesson.

When signing up to take part in the study, all participants were informed that the contents of the lesson would be made available to researchers in an anonymised way, but to avoid divulging personally identifying information, or other information they did not wish to be made public. A reminder to this effect was displayed at the start of every chatroom lesson. As an extra precaution, we made anonymisation one part of the transcription annotation procedure; see the next section for further detail.

Eight students have so far been recruited to take part in the chatroom English lessons which form this corpus. All students participated in at least 2 lessons each (max=32, mean=12). Therefore one possible use of the corpus is to study longitudinal pedagogical effects and development of second language proficiency in written English chat. At the time of data collection, the students were aged 12 to 40, with a mean of 23 years. Their first languages are Japanese (2), Ukrainian (2), Italian, Mandarin Chinese, Spanish, and Thai.

We considered being prescriptive about the format of the one-hour lessons, but in the end decided to allow the teachers to use their teaching experience and expertise to guide the content and planning of lessons. This was an extra way of discovering how teachers structure lessons and respond to individual needs, while also observing what additional resources they call on (other websites, images, source texts, etc). When signing up to participate in the study, the students were able to express their preferences for topics and skills to focus on, information which was passed on to the teachers in order that they could prepare lesson content accordingly. Since most students return for several lessons with the teachers, we can also observe how the teachers guide them through the unwritten 'curriculum' of learning English, and how students respond to this long-term treatment.

4 Annotation

The 102 collected lesson transcriptions have been annotated by an experienced teacher and examiner of English. The transcriptions were presented as spreadsheets, with each turn of the conversation as a new row, and columns for annotation values. There were several steps to the annotation process, listed and described below.

Anonymisation: As a first step before any further annotation was performed, we replaced personal names with ⟨TEACHER⟩ or ⟨STUDENT⟩ placeholders as appropriate to protect the privacy of teacher and student participants. For the same reason we replaced other sensitive data such as a date-of-birth, address, telephone number or email address with ⟨DOB⟩, ⟨ADDRESS⟩, ⟨TELEPHONE⟩, ⟨EMAIL⟩. Finally, any personally identifying information – the mention of a place of

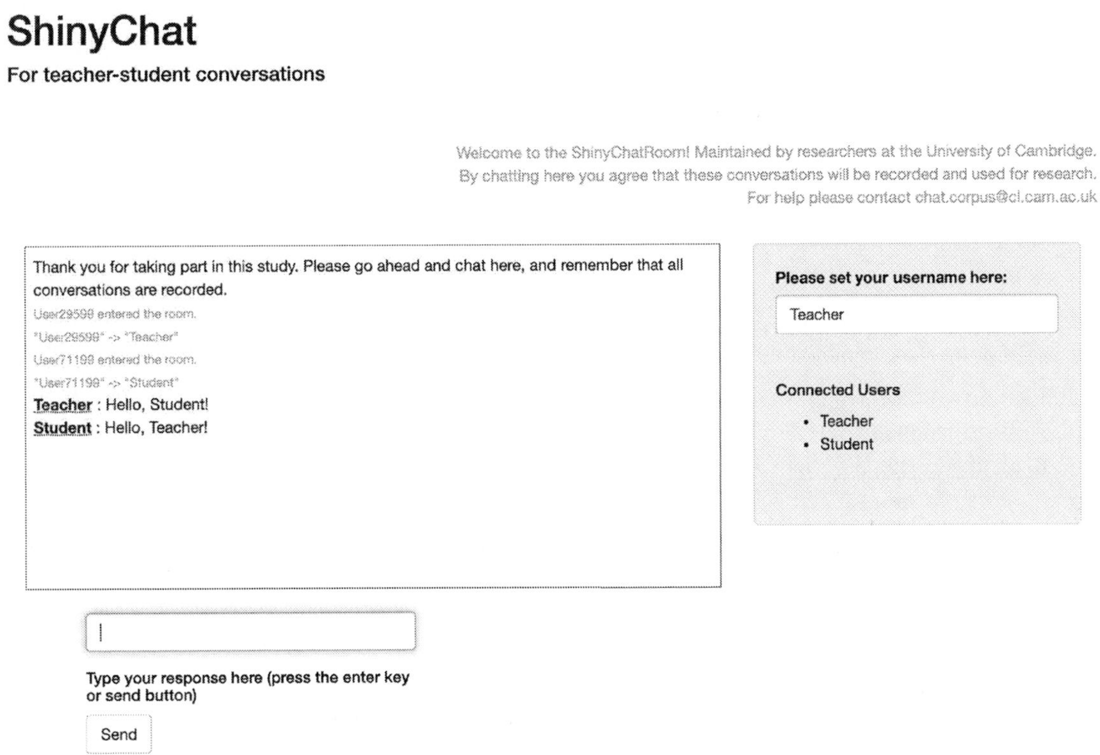

Figure 1: Screenshot of the 'ShinyChat' chatroom

work or study, description of a regular pattern of behaviour, *etc* – was removed if necessary.

Grammatical error correction: As well as the original turns of each participant, we also provide grammatically corrected versions of the student turns. The teachers make errors too, which is interesting in itself, but the focus of teaching is on the students and therefore we economise effort by correcting student turns only. The process includes grammatical errors, typos, and improvements to lexical choice. This was done in a minimal fashion to stay as close to the original meaning as possible. In addition, there can often be many possible corrections for any one grammatical error, a known problem in corpus annotation and NLP work on grammatical errors (Bryant and Ng, 2015). The usual solution is to collect multiple annotations, which we have not yet done, but plan to. In the meantime, the error annotation is useful for grammatical error *detection* even if *correction* might be improved by more annotation.

Responding to: This step involves the disentangling of conversational turns so that it was clear which preceding turn was being addressed, if it was not the previous one. As will be familiar from messaging scenarios, people can have conversations in non-linear ways, sometimes referring back to a turn long before the present one. For example, the teacher might write something in turn number 1, then something else in turn 2. In turn 3 the student responds to turn 2 – the previous one, and therefore an unmarked occurrence – but in turn 4 they respond to turn 1. The conversation 'adjacency pairs' are thus non-linear, being 1&4, 2&3.

Sequence type: We indicate major and minor shifts in conversational sequences – sections of interaction with a particular purpose, even if that purpose is from time-to-time more social than it is educational. Borrowing key concepts from the CONVERSATION ANALYSIS (CA) approach (Sacks et al., 1974), we seek out groups of turns which together represent the building blocks of the chat transcript: teaching actions which build the structure of the lessons.

> CA practitioners aim 'to discover how participants understand and respond to one another in their turns at talk, with a central focus on how *sequences of action* are generated' (Seedhouse (2004) quoting Hutchby and Wooffitt (1988),

emphasis added).

We define a number of sequence types listed and described below, firstly the major and then the minor types, or 'sub-sequences':

- Opening – greetings at the start of a conversation; may also be found mid-transcript, if for example the conversation was interrupted and conversation needs to recommence.
- Topic ___ – relates to the topic of conversation (minor labels complete this sequence type).
- Exercise – signalling the start of a constrained language exercise (*e.g.* 'please look at textbook page 50', 'let's look at the graph', *etc*); can be controlled or freer practice (*e.g.* gap-filling versus prompted re-use).
- Redirection – managing the conversation flow to switch from one topic or task to another.
- Disruption – interruption to the flow of conversation for some reason; for example because of loss of internet connectivity, telephone call, a cat stepping across the keyboard, and so on...
- Homework – the setting of homework for the next lesson, usually near the end of the present lesson.
- Closing – appropriate linguistic exchange to signal the end of a conversation.

  Below we list our minor sequence types, which complement the major sequence types:

  - Topic opening – starting a new topic: will usually be a new sequence.
  - Topic development – developing the current topic: will usually be a new sub-sequence.
  - Topic closure – a sub-sequence which brings the current topic to a close.
  - Presentation – (usually the teacher) presenting or explaining a linguistic skill or knowledge component.
  - Eliciting – (usually the teacher) continuing to seek out a particular response or realisation by the student.
  - Scaffolding – (usually the teacher) giving helpful support to the student.
  - Enquiry – asking for information about a specific skill or knowledge component.
  - Repair – correction of a previous linguistic sequence, usually in a previous turn, but could be within a turn; could be correction of self or other.
  - Clarification – making a previous turn clearer for the other person, as opposed to 'repair' which involves correction of mistakes.
  - Reference – reference to an external source, for instance recommending a textbook or website as a useful resource.
  - Recap – (usually the teacher) summarising a take-home message from the preceding turns.
  - Revision – (usually the teacher) revisiting a topic or task from a previous lesson.

Some of these sequence types are exemplified in Table 1.

Teaching focus: Here we note what type of knowledge is being targeted in the new conversation sequence or sub-sequence. These usually accompany the sequence types, Exercise, Presentation, Eliciting, Scaffolding, Enquiry, Repair and Revision.

- Grammatical resource – appropriate use of grammar.
- Lexical resource – appropriate and varied use of vocabulary.
- Meaning – what words and phrases mean (in specific contexts).
- Discourse management – how to be coherent and cohesive, refer to given information and introduce new information appropriately, signal discourse shifts, disagreement, and so on.
- Register – information about use of language which is appropriate for the setting, such as levels of formality, use of slang or profanity, or intercultural issues.
- Task achievement – responding to the prompt in a manner which fully meets requirements.
- Interactive communication – how to structure a conversation, take turns, acknowledge each other's contributions, and establish common ground.
- World knowledge – issues which relate to external knowledge, which might be linguistic (*e.g.* cultural or pragmatic subtleties) or not

Turn	Role	Anonymised	Corrected	Resp.to	Sequence
1	T	Hi there ⟨STUDENT⟩, all OK?	Hi there ⟨STUDENT⟩, all OK?		opening
2	S	Hi ⟨TEACHER⟩, how are you?	Hi ⟨TEACHER⟩, how are you?		
3	S	I did the exercise this morning	I did *some* exercise this morning		
4	S	I have done, I guess	I have done, I guess		repair
5	T	did is fine especially if you're focusing on the action itself	did is fine especially if you're focusing on the action itself		scaffolding
6	T	tell me about your exercise if you like!	tell me about your exercise if you like!	3	topic.dev

Table 1: Example of numbered, anonymised and annotated turns in the TSCC (where role T=teacher, S=student, and 'resp.to' means 'responding to'); the student is here chatting about physical exercise.

(they might simply be relevant to the current topic and task).

- Meta knowledge – discussion about the type of knowledge required for learning and assessment; for instance, 'there's been a shift to focus on X in teaching in recent years'.
- Typo - orthographic issues such as spelling, grammar or punctuation mistake
- Content – a repair sequence which involves a correction in meaning; for instance, Turn 1: Yes, that's fine. Turn 2: Oh wait, no, it's not correct.
- Exam practice – specific drills to prepare for examination scenarios.
- Admin – lesson management, such as 'please check your email' or 'see page 75'.

Use of resource: At times the teacher refers the student to materials in support of learning. These can be the chat itself – where the teacher asks the student to review some previous turns in that same lesson – or a textbook page, online video, social media account, or other website.

Student assessment: The annotator, a qualified and experienced examiner of the English language, assessed the proficiency level shown by the student in each lesson. Assessment was applied according to the Common European Framework of Reference for Languages (CEFR)[2], with levels from A1 (least advanced) to C2 (most advanced). We anticipated that students would get more out of the lessons if they were already at a fairly good level, and therefore aimed our recruitment of participants at the intermediate level and above (CEFR B1 upwards). Assessment was applied in a holistic way based on the student's turns in each lesson: evaluating use of language (grammar and vocabulary), coherence, discourse management and interaction.

[2] https://www.cambridgeenglish.org/exams-and-tests/cefr

Section	Lessons	Conv.turns	Words
Teachers	102	7632	93,602
Students	102	5920	39,293
All	102	13,552	132,895

Table 2: Number of lessons, conversational turns and words in the TSCC contributed by teachers, students and all combined.

Section	Lessons	Conv.turns	Words
B1	36	1788	11,898
B2	37	2394	11,331
C1	29	1738	16,064
Students	102	5920	39,293

Table 3: Number of lessons, conversational turns and words in the TSCC grouped by CEFR level.

In Table 1 we exemplify many of the annotation steps described above with an excerpt from the corpus. We show several anonymised turns from one of the lessons, with turn numbers, participant role, error correction, 'responding to' when not the immediately preceding turn, and sequence type labels. Other labels such as teaching focus and use of resource are in the files but not shown

		FCE	CrowdED	TSCC
Edit type	Missing	21.0%	13.9%	18.2%
	Replacement	64.4%	47.9%	72.3%
	Unnecessary	11.5%	38.2%	9.5%
Error type	Adjective	1.4%	0.8%	1.5%
	Adjective:form	0.3%	0.06%	0.1%
	Adverb	1.9%	1.5%	1.6%
	Conjunction	0.7%	1.3%	0.2%
	Contraction	0.3%	0.4%	0.1%
	Determiner	10.9%	4.0%	12.4%
	Morphology	1.9%	0.6%	2.4%
	Noun	4.6%	5.8%	9.0%
	Noun:inflection	0.5%	0.01%	0.1%
	Noun:number	3.3%	1.0%	2.1%
	Noun:possessive	0.5%	0.1%	0.03%
	Orthography	2.9%	3.0%	6.7%
	Other	13.3%	61.0%	28.4%
	Particle	0.3%	0.5%	0.6%
	Preposition	11.2%	2.9%	7.4%
	Pronoun	3.5%	1.2%	2.9%
	Punctuation	9.7%	8.7%	0.9%
	Spelling	9.6%	0.3%	6.0%
	Verb	7.0%	3.1%	6.7%
	Verb:form	3.6%	0.4%	2.9%
	Verb:inflection	0.2%	0.01%	0.1%
	Verb:subj-verb-agr	1.5%	0.3%	1.8%
	Verb:tense	6.0%	1.1%	4.8%
	Word order	1.8%	1.2%	1.0%
Corpus stats	Texts	1244	1108	102
	Words	531,416	39,726	132,895
	Total edits	52,671	8454	3800

Table 4: The proportional distribution of error types determined by grammatical error correction of texts in the TSCC. Proportions supplied for the FCE Corpus for comparison, from Bryant et al. (2019), and a subset of the CrowdED Corpus (for a full description of error types see Bryant et al. (2017))

here. The example is not exactly how the corpus texts are formatted, but it serves to illustrate: the README distributed with the corpus further explains the contents of each annotated chat file.

The annotation of the features described above may in the long-term enable improved dialogue systems for language learning, and for the moment we view them as a first small step towards that larger goal. We do not yet know which features will be most useful and relevant for training such dialogue systems, but that is the purpose of collecting wide-ranging annotation. The corpus size is still relatively small, and so for the time being they allow us to focus on the analysis of one-to-one chat lessons and understand how such lessons are structured by both teacher and student.

5 Corpus analysis

In Table 2 we report the overall statistics for TSCC in terms of lessons, conversational turns, and number of words (counted as white-space delimited tokens). We also show these statistics for the teacher and student groups separately. It is unsurprising that the teachers contribute many more turns and words to the chats than their students, but perhaps surprising just how much more they contribute. Each lesson was approximately one hour long and amounted to an average of 1300 words.

In Table 3 we show these same statistics for the student group only, and this time subsetting the

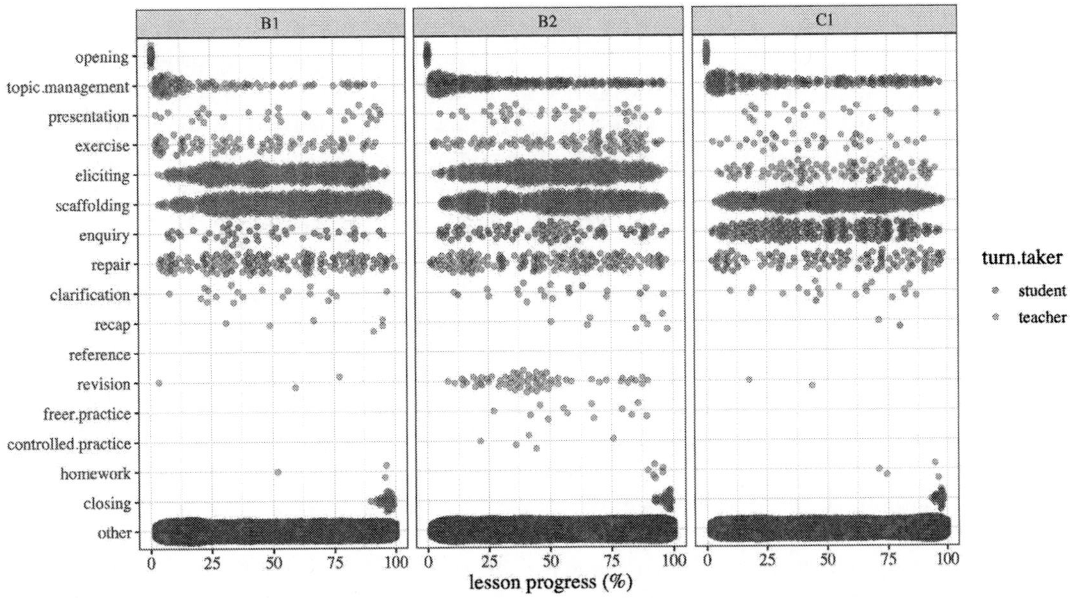

Figure 2: Selected sequence types in the TSCC, one plot per CEFR level, teachers as blue points, students as red; types on the y-axis and lesson progress on the x-axis (%). 'Other' represents all non-sequence-starting turns in the corpus.

group by the CEFR levels found in the corpus: B1, B2 and C1. As expected, no students were deemed to be of CEFR level A1 or A2 in their written English, and the majority were of the intermediate B1 and B2 levels. It is notable that the B2 students in the corpus contribute many more turns than their B1 counterparts, but fewer words. The C1 students – the least numerous group – contribute the fewest turns of all groups but by far the most words. All the above might well be explained by individual variation and/or by teacher task and topic selection (*e.g.* setting tasks which do or do not invite longer responses) per the notion of 'opportunity of use' – what skills the students get the chance to demonstrate depends on the linguistic opportunities they are given (Caines and Buttery, 2017). Certainly we did find that student performance varied from lesson to lesson, so that the student might be B2 in one lesson for instance, and B1 or C1 in others. In future work, we wish to systematically examine the interplay between lesson structure, teaching feedback and student performance, because at present we can only observe that performance may vary from lesson to lesson.

The grammatical error correction performed on student turns in TSCC enables subsequent analysis of error types. We align each student turn with its corrected version, and then type the differences found according to the error taxonomy of Bryant et al. (2017) and using the ERRANT program[3]. We then count the number of instances of each error type and present them, following Bryant et al. (2019), as major edit types ('missing', 'replacement' and 'unnecessary' words) and grammatical error types which relate more to parts-of-speech and the written form. To show how TSCC compares to other error-annotated corpora, in Table 4 we present equivalent error statistics for the FCE Corpus of English exam essays at B1 or B2 level (Yannakoudakis et al., 2011) and the CROWDED Corpus of exam-like speech monologues by native and non-native speakers of English (Caines et al., 2016).

It is apparent in Table 4 that in terms of the distribution of edits and errors the TSCC is more alike to another written corpus, the FCE, than it is to a speech corpus (CROWDED). For instance, there are far fewer 'unnecessary' edit types in the TSCC than in CROWDED, with the majority being 'replacement' edit types like the FCE. For the error types, there is a smaller catch-all 'other' category for TSCC than CROWDED, along with many determiner, noun and preposition errors in common with FCE. There is a focus on the written form, with many orthography and spelling errors, but far fewer punctuation errors than the other cor-

[3]`https://github.com/chrisjbryant/errant`

pora – a sign that chat interaction has almost no standard regarding punctuation.

In Figure 2 we show where selected sequence types begin as points in the progress of each lesson (expressed as percentages) and which participant begins them, the teacher or student. Opening and closing sequences are where we might expect them at the beginning and end of lessons. The bulk of topic management occurs at the start of lessons and the bulk of eliciting and scaffolding occurs mid-lesson. Comparing the different CEFR levels, there are many fewer exercise and eliciting sequences for the C1 students compared to the B1 and B2 students; in contrast the C1 students do much more enquiry. In future work we aim to better analyse the scaffolding, repair and revision sequences in particular, to associate them with relevant preceding turns and understand what prompted the onset of these particular sequences.

6 Conclusion

We have described the Teacher-Student Chatroom Corpus, which we believe to be the first resource of its kind available for research use, potentially enabling both close discourse analysis and the eventual development of educational technology for practice in written English conversation. It currently contains 102 one-to-one lessons between two teachers and eight students of various ages and backgrounds, totalling 133K words, along with annotation for a range of linguistic and pedagogic features. We demonstrated how such annotation enables new insight into the language teaching process, and propose that in future the dataset can be used to inform dialogue system design, in a similar way to Höhn's work with the German-language deL1L2IM corpus (Höhn, 2017).

One possible outcome of this work is to develop an engaging chatbot which is able to perform a limited number of language teaching tasks based on pedagogical expertise and insights gained from the TSCC. The intention is not to replace human teachers, but the chatbot can for example lighten the load of running a lesson – taking the 'easier' administrative tasks such as lesson opening and closing, or homework-setting – allowing the teacher to focus more on pedagogical aspects, or to multi-task across several lessons at once. This would be a kind of human-in-the-loop dialogue system or, from the teacher's perspective, assistive technology which can bridge between high quality but non-scalable one-to-one tutoring, and the current limitations of natural language processing technology. Such educational technology can bring the benefit of personalised tutoring, for instance reducing the anxiety of participating in group discussion (Griffin and Roy, 2019), while also providing the implicit skill and sensitivity brought by experienced human teachers.

First though, we need to demonstrate that (a) such a CALL system would be a welcome innovation for learners and teachers, and that (b) chatroom lessons do benefit language learners. We have seen preliminary evidence for both, but it remains anecdotal and a matter for thorough investigation in future. Collecting more data of the type described here will allow us to more comprehensively cover different teaching styles, demographic groups and L1 backgrounds. At the moment any attempt to look at individual variation can only be that: our group sizes are not yet large enough to be representative. We also aim to better understand the teaching actions contained in our corpus, how feedback sequences relate to the preceding student turns, and how the student responds to this feedback both within the lesson and across lessons over time.

Acknowledgments

This paper reports on research supported by Cambridge Assessment, University of Cambridge. Additional funding was provided by the Cambridge Language Sciences Research Incubator Fund and the Isaac Newton Trust. We thank Jane Walsh, Jane Durkin, Reka Fogarasi, Mark Brenchley, Mark Cresham, Kate Ellis, Tanya Hall, Carol Nightingale and Joy Rook for their support. We are grateful to the teachers, students and annotators without whose enthusiastic participation this corpus would not have been feasible.

References

Sherrie Atwood, William Turnbull, and Jeremy I. M. Carpendale. 2010. The construction of knowledge in classroom talk. *Journal of the Learning Sciences*, 19(3):358–402.

Douglas Biber, Susan Conrad, Randi Reppen, Pat Byrd, Marie Helt, Victoria Clark, Viviana Cortes, Eniko Csomay, and Alfredo Urzua. 2004. *Representing language use in the university: Analysis of the TOEFL 2000 spoken and written academic language corpus*. Princeton, NJ: Educational Testing Service.

BNC Consortium. 2001. The British National Corpus, version 2 (BNC World).

Christopher Bryant, Mariano Felice, Øistein Andersen, and Ted Briscoe. 2019. The BEA-2019 Shared Task on Grammatical Error Correction. In *Proceedings of the Fourteenth Workshop on Innovative Use of NLP for Building Educational Applications (BEA)*.

Christopher Bryant, Mariano Felice, and Ted Briscoe. 2017. Automatic annotation and evaluation of error types for grammatical error correction. In *Proceedings of the 55th Annual Meeting of the Association for Computational Linguistics (Volume 1: Long Papers)*.

Christopher Bryant and Hwee Tou Ng. 2015. How far are we from fully automatic high quality grammatical error correction? In *Proceedings of the 53rd Annual Meeting of the Association for Computational Linguistics and the 7th International Joint Conference on Natural Language Processing (Volume 1: Long Papers)*.

Paweł Budzianowski, Tsung-Hsien Wen, Bo-Hsiang Tseng, Iñigo Casanueva, Stefan Ultes, Osman Ramadan, and Milica Gašić. 2018. MultiWOZ - a large-scale multi-domain Wizard-of-Oz dataset for task-oriented dialogue modelling. In *Proceedings of the 2018 Conference on Empirical Methods in Natural Language Processing*.

Andrew Caines, Christian Bentz, Dimitrios Alikaniotis, Fridah Katushemererwe, and Paula Buttery. 2016. The glottolog data explorer: Mapping the world's languages. In *Proceedings of the LREC 2016 Workshop 'VisLR II: Visualization as Added Value in the Development, Use and Evaluation of Language Resources'*.

Andrew Caines and Paula Buttery. 2017. The effect of task and topic on language use in learner corpora. In Lynne Flowerdew and Vaclav Brezina, editors, *Written and spoken learner corpora and their use in different contexts*. London: Bloomsbury.

Ronald Carter and Michael McCarthy. 1997. *Exploring Spoken English*. Cambridge: Cambridge University Press.

Winston Chang, Joe Cheng, JJ Allaire, Yihui Xie, and Jonathan McPherson. 2020. *shiny: Web Application Framework for R*. R package version 1.4.0.2.

Eniko Csomay. 2012. Lexical Bundles in Discourse Structure: A Corpus-Based Study of Classroom Discourse. *Applied Linguistics*, 34(3):369–388.

Cristian Danescu-Niculescu-Mizil and Lillian Lee. 2011. Chameleons in imagined conversations: A new approach to understanding coordination of linguistic style in dialogs. In *Proceedings of the 2nd Workshop on Cognitive Modeling and Computational Linguistics*.

Mihail Eric, Rahul Goel, Shachi Paul, Abhishek Sethi, Sanchit Agarwal, Shuyang Gao, Adarsh Kumar, Anuj Goyal, Peter Ku, and Dilek Hakkani-Tur. 2020. MultiWOZ 2.1: A consolidated multi-domain dialogue dataset with state corrections and state tracking baselines. In *Proceedings of The 12th Language Resources and Evaluation Conference*.

Jane Evison. 2013. Turn openings in academic talk: where goals and roles intersect. *Classroom Discourse*, 4(1):3–26.

Lynda Griffin and James Roy. 2019. A great resource that should be utilised more, but also a place of anxiety: student perspectives on using an online discussion forum. *Open Learning: The Journal of Open, Distance and e-Learning*, pages 1–16.

Sviatlana Höhn. 2017. A data-driven model of explanations for a chatbot that helps to practice conversation in a foreign language. In *Proceedings of the 18th Annual SIGdial Meeting on Discourse and Dialogue*.

Ian Hutchby and Robin Wooffitt. 1988. *Conversation analysis*. Cambridge: Polity Press.

Robbie Love, Claire Dembry, Andrew Hardie, Vaclav Brezina, and Tony McEnery. 2017. The Spoken BNC2014: designing and building a spoken corpus of everyday conversations. *International Journal of Corpus Linguistics*, 22:319–344.

Anne O'Keeffe and Steve Walsh. 2012. Applying corpus linguistics and conversation analysis in the investigation of small group teaching in higher education. *Corpus Linguistics and Linguistic Theory*, 8:159–181.

Alan Ritter, Colin Cherry, and Bill Dolan. 2010. Unsupervised modeling of Twitter conversations. In *Human Language Technologies: The 2010 Annual Conference of the North American Chapter of the Association for Computational Linguistics*.

Stephen Roller, Emily Dinan, Naman Goyal, Da Ju, Mary Williamson, Yinhan Liu, Jing Xu, Myle Ott, Kurt Shuster, Eric M. Smith, Y-Lan Boureau, and Jason Weston. 2020. Recipes for building an open-domain chatbot. *arXiv*, 2004.13637.

Carolyn P. Rosé, Diane Litman, Dumisizwe Bhembe, Kate Forbes, Scott Silliman, Ramesh Srivastava, and Kurt VanLehn. 2003. A comparison of tutor and student behavior in speech versus text based tutoring. In *Proceedings of the HLT-NAACL 03 Workshop on Building Educational Applications Using Natural Language Processing*.

Harvey Sacks, Emanuel Schegloff, and Gail Jefferson. 1974. A simplest systematics for the organization of turn-taking for conversation. *Language*, 50:696–735.

Nicolas Schrading, Cecilia Ovesdotter Alm, Ray Ptucha, and Christopher Homan. 2015. An analysis of domestic abuse discourse on Reddit. In *Proceedings of the 2015 Conference on Empirical Methods in Natural Language Processing*.

Paul Seedhouse. 2004. Conversation analysis methodology. *Language Learning*, 54:1–54.

Rita Simpson, Susan Briggs, John Ovens, and John Swales. 2002. *Michigan Corpus of Academic Spoken English*. Ann Arbor: University of Michigan.

Katherine Stasaski, Kimberly Kao, and Marti A. Hearst. 2020. CIMA: A large open access dialogue dataset for tutoring. In *Proceedings of the Fifteenth Workshop on Innovative Use of NLP for Building Educational Applications*.

Etsuko Toyoda and Richard Harrison. 2002. Categorization of text chat communication between learners and native speakers of Japanese. *Language Learning Technology*, 6:82–99.

Helen Yannakoudakis, Ted Briscoe, and Ben Medlock. 2011. A new dataset and method for automatically grading ESOL texts. In *Proceedings of the 49th Annual Meeting of the Association for Computational Linguistics: Human Language Technologies*.

Polygloss - A conversational agent for language practice

Etiene da Cruz Dalcol
Queen Mary University
London, UK
dalcol@etiene.net

Massimo Poesio
Queen Mary University
London, UK
m.poesio@qmul.ac.uk

Abstract

This paper explores the impact on language proficiency of comprehensible output applied in computer assisted language learning (CALL). Targeting speakers of intermediate level, we adapted a visually-grounded dialogue task, optimizing for language acquisition. The task was implemented as a mobile application where learners are organized in pairs and write short texts to play an image-guessing game, producing samples in a wide variety of languages. Following a framework for CALL evaluation, we conducted an analysis of the game and players' gains through time, including the measure of pre-trained XLM-r cross-lingual transformers' acceptability score of the samples. The results confirm the intended fit for intermediate speakers as well as reveal possible benefits for other levels. This research provides a successful case study of a multilingual CALL design where users have the autonomy to generate output creatively.

1 Introduction

Reaching high proficiency levels and being successful at interacting with others is the ultimate goal of many adult intermediate learners of a second language. There are, however, many obstacles along this journey, related to strategies chosen by self-directed learners, accessibility of learning materials, and the influences of the natural plateau found at the higher end of the learning curve (Ritter and Schooler, 2001).

Once a learner has reached an intermediate proficiency, they have learned the most frequent words. It can then be a struggle to jump over to the next stage because only a small number of words are very frequent and the frequency quickly drops for the following words, creating an extremely long-tailed curve. Sparsity is even more of an issue when we consider that one of the features of advanced speech to be acquired are collocations. Nevertheless, when learners can understand 80-95% of the words, they can infer a lot of words through the context, causing many students to abandon active study and focus on passive consumption of foreign media. However, there is not enough repetition of the advanced vocabulary that the student needs to learn for it to become part of the productive vocabulary (Nation and Hunston, 2013). This manifests as a much higher receptive vocabulary than a productive vocabulary, the "I can understand but I cannot speak" phase.

Notwithstanding this consensus that conversational practice is essential to go beyond this phase, most commercial language learning apps do not support conversational practice and are usually only available for the most popular languages.

In this paper we propose Polygloss, a game to provide conversational practice to intermediate level learners. While not intended to tackle all the skills necessary to overcome the language learning plateau, Polygloss draws on principles from critical pedagogy (Freire, 1972) to tackle an often neglected skill, *creative production*. We investigate and highlight its importance to overall language proficiency. At the same time, we want to do that by providing a free tool that is sufficiently general and does not sideline learners of less spoken languages.

2 Background

2.1 Comprehensible Output and Languaging

As a counterpoint to the input hypothesis (Krashen and Terrell, 1983), which argues that being exposed to vast amounts of input alone is neces-

This work is licensed under a Creative Commons Attribution 4.0 International Licence. Licence details: http://creativecommons.org/licenses/by/4.0/.

Etiene da Cruz Dalcol and Massimo Poesio 2020. Polygloss – A conversational agent for language practice. *Proceedings of the 9th Workshop on Natural Language Processing for Computer Assisted Language Learning (NLP4CALL 2020).* Linköping Electronic Conference Proceedings 175: 21–36.

sary for language acquisition[1], without denying the role of input, Swain (1985), argues that comprehensible output is also necessary. The main function of *Comprehensible Output* is allowing the students to notice their gaps when they realize what they cannot say, testing hypothesis on interlocutors, and improving fluency by gaining self-confidence. While her early work is more focused on "pushed" output, where the teacher encourages students to produce language, her later work goes deeper into interaction. Influenced by Vygotsky's sociocultural theory of mind and the *Zone of Proximal Development* (ZPD) (Vygotsky, 1978), she adopted a new term, *Languaging*, to describe the "shaping and organizing of higher mental processes through language use" (Swain, 2006).

2.2 Critical Pedagogy in the future of CALL

While ZPD is informed by Piaget's theory of children being autonomous learners, it is still founded on the mediation between a student and a more knowledgeable peer or teacher. By contrast, our work was founded on Freire's method for adult literacy (Freire, 1972), a cornerstone work for the field of critical pedagogy. Freire does not place the participation of the teacher as a superior or even as a fundamental part of the learning process, but argues instead for a learning methodology centered on the student's development of agency for the purpose of reshaping social structures of power. The process starts with a search for *charged words* during an informal chat with the students using images to facilitate the discussion (see Fig. 1). The elicited vocabulary is then used to generate debate themes that allow the students to talk about their day-to-day, explore their identities and argue their beliefs. Freire's work has influenced much socially-informed work in second language acquisition (Saft et al., 2001; Anya, 2016; Benson, 2013).

Within Computer Assisted Language Learning, Benson (2013) re-frames Warschauer's stages of CALL history (Warschauer, 1996) under the perspective of user control. He notes that intelligent CALL (iCALL), powered by artificial intelligence, is often regarded as the future of CALL. However, it can still stripe users of autonomy as designers of such systems can view autonomy as undesired or even problematic. He suggests the interesting innovations will focus on self-directed learning and the development of autonomy.

[1]While Krashen makes a distinction, in this paper we use the terms *learning* and *acquisition* interchangeably.

Figure 1: Two illustrations by Vicente de Abreu used in Paulo Freire's curriculum (Freire, 1967)

3 Related work

In a recent overview of the sub-field of dialogue-based CALL, Bibauw et al. (2019) review the field focusing on work where an automated system is one of the interlocutors. Although most work on computer mediated communication (CMC) is focused on written text technologies such as Wikis and Email, and employed qualitative but not quantitative methods (Macaro et al., 2012), there are nevertheless a number of relevant research papers and commercial applications we would like to mention.

WUFUN (Ma and Kelly, 2006) and TESU (Liu et al., 2014) are vocabulary trainers focused on communicative competence that go through an end-to-end analysis from theory to quantitative evaluation on the users productive vocabulary. Spanish Without Walls (Blake, 2005) is a learning program that employs a CMC application for audio and text, highlighting the importance of such tools in the context of distance learning. These applications were dedicated to teaching a single language, but MagicWord (Hatier et al., 2019), offers a multilingual word game, initially developed for Italian, French and English. Revita (Katinskaia et al., 2017) is a system with automated fill-the-gap exercises for stimulating active vocabulary. While it is proposed for endangered languages, it faces various challenges related to its multilingualism such as the lack of corpora. CALL-SLT (Rayner et al., 2010) is a system that uses a textual or pictorial representation of an interlingua to prompt users' speech in four supported second languages. Despite facing challenges like limited vocabulary, its recognition and feedback steps are done by an underlying automated agent which was well-received by the players.

In the field of commercial mobile applications for language learning, we inspected many and perceived them as belonging to distinct groups, according to their approach: those with a tutoring approach such as Duolingo, Memrise, Busuu, Babbel, Rosetta Stone, Ling and Mango Languages; those focused on vocabulary games such as Drops, Clozemaster, LyricsTraining and Lingvist; those focused on providing comprehensible input such as LingQ, FluentU, Beelinguapp and Yabla; those focused on conversations with other learners and natives such as HelloTalk and Tandem; and chatbots such as Andy.

With the exception of the apps in the last two groups, they usually do not allow the user to create their own authentic outputs, expecting fixed responses deemed correct for exercises such as translating, sentence restructuring or fill-the-gap. Nevertheless, the Andy chatbot, while technically giving the user freedom, is limited to English and often fails to process the text provided by users. HelloTalk and Tandem are essentially chatting apps with added useful features such as correction tools. This divides the domain in applications where you either have no interaction with other interlocutors at all, or applications for advanced communication with full conversations, unguided and unstructured.

4 Polygloss, a conversational agent for language practice

The Polygloss application is an adaptation of the PhotoBook task (Haber et al., 2019) for the domain of Computer Assisted Language Learning (CALL). The PhotoBook task was created to study how people build and accumulate common ground through crowd-sourced visually-grounded dialogue. It ran on Amazon Mechanical Turk and consisted of displaying 6 images to the participants and letting them talk to each other until they figured out which images they had in common.

Our application draws on the design of this task and Freire's methodology (Freire, 1972), still using images to give users something to talk about, but making adjustments and simplifications to encourage language acquisition. The main difference is that, while PhotoBook collects data exclusively in English, Polygloss lets users pick any language they would like to learn. Another important difference is that our experiment did not run on Amazon Mechanical Turk, but rather as a free downloadable mobile application for the Android operating system, in order to capture users that are actively learning a language.

4.1 System architecture

Because of its turn-taking characteristic, mobile was picked as a more appropriate distribution platform for the application since it offers easy functions for notifying users. The programming language and development framework used were Dart and Flutter[2], instead of Java, due to their capability to compile for multiple operating systems. So far, the application can only run on phones running the Android operating system, but it could also be published to the iOS App Store in the future.

The game was built with a "serverless" architecture. The only code written for the game was the application installed in the users' phones, which acts a client application. It connects directly to the database that stores the game history and settings, the user authentication service, the image storage service, and the analytics service, provided by Google Cloud Platform[3], through HTTP requests to their API, as seen on Fig. 2. We do not have our own back-end, which significantly reduces maintenance work.

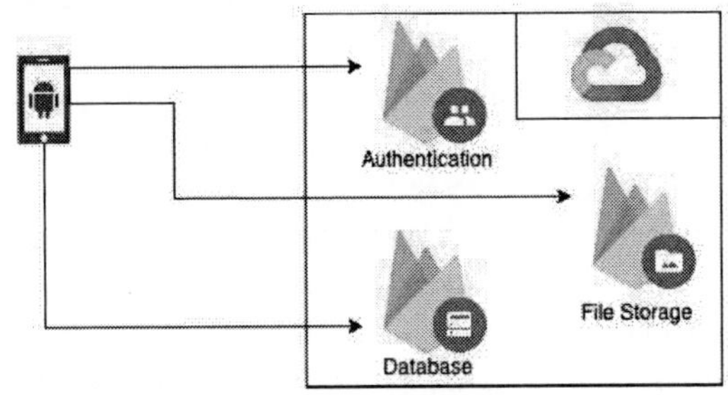

Figure 2: Architecture of API requests to Cloud Services

The game was then published to the Android Play Store, which allows an easy distribution of the software and its updates to the users, plus a set of useful development tools such as staged deployments, and collection of application feedback, statistics and errors.

[2]https://flutter.dev/

[3]https://cloud.google.com/

4.2 Design of the application

Since a match can be in any language, the user-pairing possibility is sparser: having two users willing to play in the same language at the same time is a rare event. In order to mitigate that, the matches have a shorter duration, using small texts instead of long dialogues, in comparison with the PhotoBook task, and are played asynchronously, i.e. in turns. The users get a notification on their mobile phone once they have a response or an invitation for a match and it is their turn. That means that Polygloss does not collect a dataset with the same utility as PhotoBook, since the samples produced are not full dialogues, but it still collects visually grounded short texts which could be useful for various goals such as image labelling or enriching word embeddings with more context. It also collects proportionally more learner language, which can be used to obtain insights into second language acquisition or to improve applications that fail to work with non-native speakers. Since the language option is open, there is also possibility for collecting native samples from various languages or dialects which are under resourced, such as South Tyrolean German.

The images used in Polygloss were sourced from a catalogue of illustrations[4], for which a license was purchased. In order to add an educational component, the images were manually curated to be simple, displaying usually one object or action, and were divided into categories such as "Hobbies", "Animals", "Emotions", defining the lessons, each containing between 10 and 60 images. There are 104 lessons in total, which increase in difficulty, for which the user has to collect "stars" to unlock and progress through, as seen on Fig. 3. The theme and order of the lessons was chosen based on common topics engaged by educational materials. The materials consulted were 7 different textbooks and websites destined to A1 - B2 students of German, Spanish, Greek and Brazilian Portuguese.

When the player finishes completing their profile, they are given a new match suggestion. For the new match, the app has to make three decisions: in which language will the next match be played, what lesson is selected, and who will be the opponent. The language is chosen among the ones that the player has declared in their profile, their native or mastered languages included. There

[4]https://www.flaticon.com

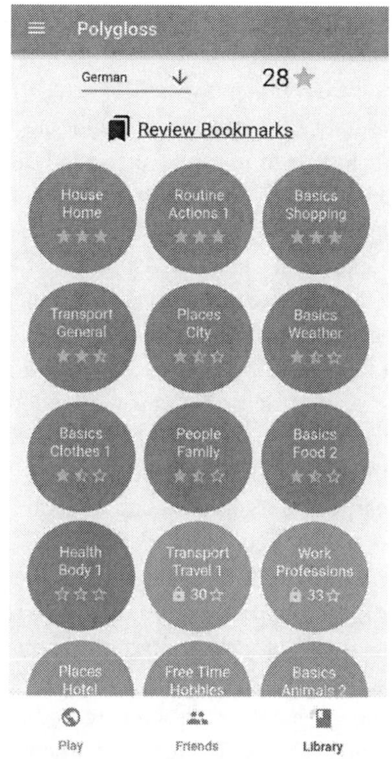

Figure 3: Screen showing Library tab containing the lesson tree

is an 80% chance that the language selected will be a language that the user is interested in learning, and a 20% chance that it is a language that they already speak. The application then analyses the player's history of played lessons to decide what lesson will be started. Lessons where the player already has three stars or that require more stars to be unlocked than the player has currently accumulated are discarded. One lesson is then chosen randomly from the remaining ones. A series of queries and filtering is done to select the opponent. First they are filtered on basis of the language chosen. If the initial player is a learner, the selected opponent can be either another learner or a speaker. If the original player is a speaker, other speakers are discarded as opponents. Subsequent filtering is done to retain more active players and exclude players who have been blocked by the user.

Once the match is started, the initial player is shown 4 random images picked from the collection of images in the lesson and one of them is selected. Then they are assigned with the task of helping their opponent guess which image is selected by writing a short text. One reason why we display 4 images, instead of 6 used in PhotoBook, is that we felt it was still enough variety to offer context while having a more appropriate fit to the typical screen size mobile phones. After the initial player finishes their turn, a notification is sent to the opponent and then they can respond to the match and select the correct image, using the language toolbar if they wish, or not, as shown on Fig. 4. If they pick the correct one, they are awarded points which count towards their number of stars. The rounds are then reversed, and it is time for the opponent to be shown a selected image and help the initial player with a short text. In this way, both players have the opportunity to practice creative language output and are receiving input. Other features of Polygloss aimed for helping language students are present in the toolbar: tools to work with the text from their partners like Copy, Translate and Bookmark; and the possibility to give corrective feedback, allowing players to negotiate meaning and modify their round's text after the feedback received.

Figure 4: Screen showing second round of match, containing text, toolbar and image selection

5 Evaluating Polygloss for language learning

Chapelle (2001) states that CALL applications should be evaluated at three levels: the CALL software itself, the teacher-planned CALL activities, and the learners' performance during the CALL activities. She highlights 6 criteria of task appropriateness for language learning to be evaluated through a combination of judgemental and empirical methods: language learning potential, learner fit, meaning focus, authenticity, positive impact and practicality. We will discuss our results regarding these criteria throughout the next sections.

In order to investigate the efficacy of the system for language practicing, we used different automated techniques for scoring the text produced by the players, as well as conducted a user survey to inquire the players experiences during the interaction with the system.

To understand how the player is progressing over time, it is necessary to measure more than how often they succeed in the image guessing game, as improvements in conducting the task could mean simply that one got better in playing the game. It could mean getting accustomed with the user interface, observing what gives more points, or even cheating.

When applications like Duolingo, offer explicit or implicit knowledge following a certain curriculum, it is possible to test players against that knowledge and see how well they perform. Duolingo does so via checkpoint quizzes tagged with something they call "communicative component", which marks what a question tests. Doing so allows them to measure the players' evolution with very few questions.

However, during unstructured creative practice, the space of possibilities is too vast. Truly observing their language progress over time involves measuring their proficiency at different points in time. Without a progressive curriculum with which to reduce the scope of the test, we would have to conduct a thorough exam in each measuring point. That would be too labor intensive for us to prepare in the timeframe of this research, especially given the multilingual characteristic of the application. It would also overly disrupt the usual gameplay, adding long interruptions for the player. One alternative to circumvent this issue is to analyse intrinsic characteristics of the text produced by the players within the game itself, which is the approach we take in this study.

5.1 Text Quality

There are different ways in which the quality of an utterance by a non-native speaker could be measured. The Common European Framework of Reference for Languages (CEFR) states that communicative language competence can be divided into the following components: linguistic, sociolinguistic and pragmatic, each with several sub-components. The CAF framework of language proficiency (Housen et al., 2012) highlights *Complexity*, *Accuracy*, and *Fluency*. These main competences are further divided into several subcomponents and although organized in different structures, several sub-components have equivalents in both frameworks.

Given our study collects very short written texts on limited interactions, it is not possible to evaluate some of these dimensions of competence, such as phonological competence, and others would be extremely difficult to measure, such as sociocultural competence. However, in both language frameworks, each component or sub-component has its contribution to the overall language proficiency. Therefore, we will focus on a limited number of metrics, with the understanding that they contribute to the general communicative competence of the players.

Metrics of syntactic complexity have been used to indicate syntactic competence of the learners (Bhat and Yoon, 2014). As seen on Table 1, we selected 2 of such metrics to include in our study: mean length of text and mean depth of parse-tree of text. Additionally, we are using word-embeddings acceptability score as a third metric.

Word embeddings can be understood as a general class of techniques to represent the meaning of lexical units through dense vectors of real numbers. They are built with statistical or neural methods based on the co-occurrence of the units in a very large corpus of text. There is a vast range of methods used to build them, and variations on what is the base lexical unit: from character-level to whole document embeddings. These vectors have been used for language modelling (Mikolov et al., 2013), which means they are sensitive to collocations, a feature of advanced speech. One metric obtained from such models is the acceptability score, the ability of the model to predict a sample. In theory, this metric could be used to capture lexical competence and accuracy as samples with many words unrelated to each other, or containing orthographic mistakes, awkward word orders and other errors, would manifest as a lower score. At the time of writing, we were not aware of any other studies using this method specifically for measuring proficiency of language learners, but there is extensive research on how such models capture grammaticality (Lau et al., 2016) and they have been previously used to judge grammar acceptability (Warstadt et al., 2018). One caveat of this metric is that the use of extremely rare words could also result in a lower score. However, we suspect this limitation would be less significant in the context of learner language considering learners will often be using very common words and the not so frequent words they need to learn are still common enough to be well captured by such models.

Before evaluating the players over time, first we investigated how the metric themselves were behaving by dividing the sentences into groups according to the players self-declared proficiency and observing if there were any anomalies.

We used Jupyter notebooks[5] and Python 3.7 to measure the first metric, adding a Natural Language Processing library for Python called Spacy[6] for the second metric, and, for the last metric, a Machine Learning library called PyTorch[7] and XLM-RoBERTa (Lample and Conneau, 2019), a generic cross lingual sentence encoder pre-trained on 2.5T of data in 100 languages. To parse a sentence with Spacy, it is necessary to download a package for each language, which is why we restricted our dataset to the five most used ones.

5.2 User Survey

We prepared a questionnaire, sent to the players' email addresses, containing various questions regarding their interaction with the application. The main goal of the questionnaire was to tap into the perceived language learning usefulness and benefits of Polygloss. We also included questions related to its interface, user experience and entertainment value. Finally, in order to explore possible future improvements, we also had an open text field for any extra feedback or suggestions the players might have. The full questionnaire can be found on Appendix A.

[5]https://jupyter.org/
[6]https://spacy.io/
[7]https://pytorch.org/

	Metric	Evaluation
I	Text length	Syntactic Complexity
II	Depth of parse-tree	Syntactic Complexity
III	XLM-r acceptability score	Lexical Competence and Accuracy

Table 1: Metrics for text evaluation

6 Results

6.1 Polygloss in use

321 language learners from various backgrounds downloaded the application, created a profile, and played a match. During profile creation, they were asked to self-declare the proficiency level for all of the languages they speak, or are interested in learning, in 4 different levels: beginner, intermediate, advanced, and native. These levels were chosen because it was not expected from all of the players to be familiar with the CEFR (Common European Framework of Reference for Languages) scale of language proficiency (Council of Europe, 2001). Moreover, not all languages that could be declared are commonly measured according to this scale. Finally, learners' self-assessment of language skills accuracy can be considered significant (Liu and Brantmeier, 2019). We assume there is also little motivation for users to lie or exaggerate in the scenario of playing our game, unlike a scenario where, for example, one is applying for a job position that requires specific language skills when they are in dire need of a paid occupation.

The players' profiles declared over 80 different languages with various degrees of knowledge. The most popular languages were English, Spanish, French, Portuguese and German.

In a period of approximately six months, the players played 5460 matches, of which 1977 were played to completion, creating over 7000 samples of sentences or very short texts in over 40 languages and dialects. The top played languages were English, Spanish, French, German, Portuguese, Greek, Italian, Russian, Japanese and Dutch, in this order. Other languages had minor numbers, and there were very interesting samples collected, such as 35 samples in Esperanto, an artificially constructed language, and 97 samples in a dialect of German from the South Tyrol region of Italy. Because of practical reasons related to the libraries used in the evaluation, which we will discuss in the next section, we have limited our

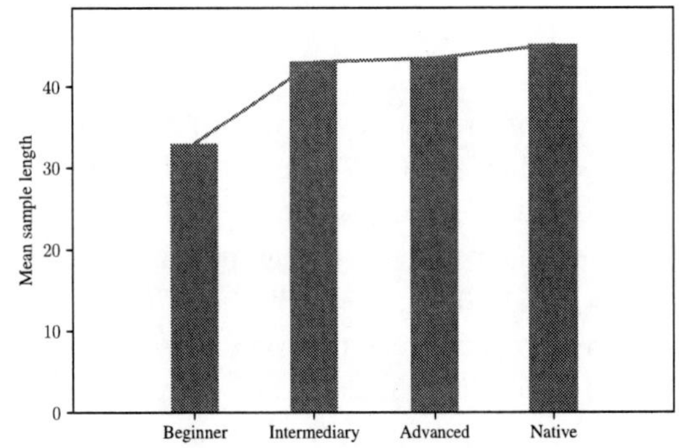

Figure 5: Mean length of sample per user group

dataset to 5276 samples created in the 5 most used languages, as seen on Table 2. The full number of samples collected can be seen on Appendix B.

6.2 Text quality among proficiency groups

6.2.1 Text length

During the initial study of the metrics, a difference of 10 characters was found between the mean length of samples produced by beginner and intermediary speakers, as seen on Fig. 5. A very small change was found between intermediary and advanced speakers, and only a slight difference of 2 characters was found in the mean between advanced and native speakers. Throughout the rest of this study, a Welch's unequal variances t-test is used to determine if differences among two groups are significant. In this case, apart from beginner (M = 32.95, SD = 18.8) versus intermediary (M = 43.03, SD = 28.57, t(2864) = -11.38, $p < 0.001$), they were not. Tests between the intermediary group and the advanced group (M = 43.48, SD = 24.05, t(3130) = -0.47, p = 0.63), or the advanced group versus native (M = 45.11, SD = 30.12, t(2353) = -1.37, p = 0.17) found no significant difference of player performance in text length.

One could argue that text length could vary according to the language, and the results could be different once breaking down. Indeed, a com-

Language	Beginner	Intermediary	Advanced	Native	Total
English	90	178	621	280	1173
Spanish	304	464	278	108	1168
German	309	454	90	173	1048
French	138	428	436	31	1035
Portuguese	349	152	31	307	852
Total	1190	1676	1456	899	5276

Table 2: Number of samples in selected languages

parison of similar levels in different languages showed they are very different, for example, beginner Spanish players (M = 38.14, SD = 22.56) wrote longer texts than beginner English players (M = 26.31, SD = 11.06, t(392) = 6.76, $p < 0.001$). After comparing each pairing of adjacent levels within each language, the full breakdown can be found on Appendix C, a wide variety of patterns emerged. Only in Portuguese could all levels be reasonably distinguished from each other, but even then, the group of intermediate speakers (M = 38.65, SD = 20.99) performed significantly better than the advanced speakers (M = 31.61, SD = 13.44), t(181) = 2.38, $p < 0.05$).

6.2.2 Depth of parse-tree

For the second metric, again the biggest difference among the proficiency groups in selected samples is between beginner and intermediary speakers, consisting of 0.26 levels in the depth of the parse tree of the samples, as seen on Fig. 6. One could make the same argument regarding differences between languages here. After comparing similar levels between languages, a consistent behaviour was not found, beginners did not vary between most language pairs, but subsequent levels often varied. Within each language sampled, in none of them it was possible to determine significant gaps between every level.

6.2.3 XLM-r acceptability score

For the last metric, before analysing the groups, a preliminary test with some example sentences, shown on Table 3, was done to observe if the scores seemed acceptable. It did not behave as expected in all instances. The example in Spanish where we compared a correct sentence and a sentence containing a grammatical error showed the error sentence as having a higher score than the correct one. The correct Spanish sentence also obtained a much lower score than the other correct

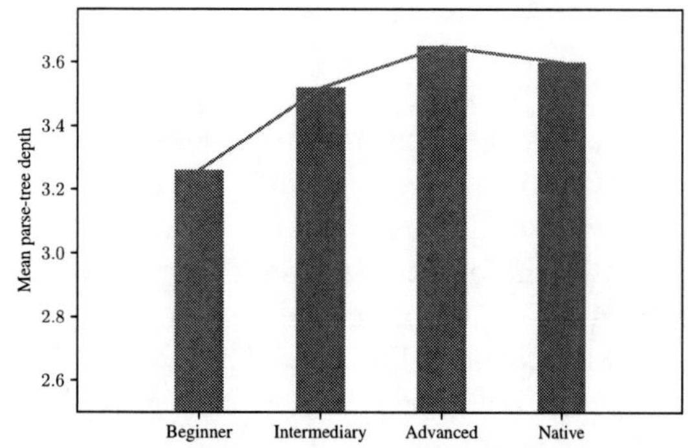

Figure 6: Mean depth of sample's parse-tree per user group

examples. It is not possible to inspect the reason in detail, but most of the examples seemed to obtain reasonable results.

Once we scored and averaged the samples in all groups, differently from the previous metrics, the biggest interval was between the intermediary and the advanced speakers, being 4.32%, as seen on Fig. 7. Given the multilingual nature of this metric, we expected no significant differences once further breaking down the groups by language, and indeed, at beginner and intermediate levels no significant difference was found between any of the language pairs. However, at subsequent levels some differences emerged, especially with advanced speakers of English, who performed better than most other groups. Overall, the difference in performance between beginner (M = 81.31, SD = 32.27) and intermediate (M = 84.08, SD = 29.72, t(2864)= -2.34, $p < 0.05$) players was significant, the difference between intermediate and advanced (M = 88.4, SD = 25.83, t(3130) = -4.34, $p < 0.001$) speakers as well, and no significant difference was found between the advanced and the native players (M= 89.62, SD = 24.19, t(2353) = -1.15, p =

Sentence	Score
This is a good sentence	99.49
This is a sentence good	4.81
C'est une bonne phrase	99.87
C'est une bone phrase	72.89
Das ist ein guter Satz	99.8
Das ist ein guter satz	98.37
Esta é uma boa frase	99.86
Esta são uma boa frase	32.85
Esta es una buena frase	83.79
Esta es un bueno frase	85.76
This is a good sentence	99.49
This is shorter	99.42
This is also a good sentence but longer	99.69
This is a wet tissue	99.85
This is a wet sentence	81.81
This is a potato sentence	30.53

Table 3: Acceptability scores on XLM-r encoders of example sentences

0.24).

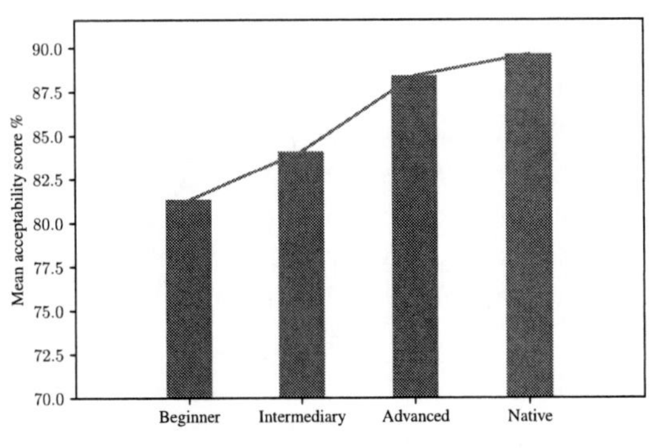

Figure 7: Mean XLM-r acceptability score per user group

6.3 Text quality over time of application usage

The average number of rounds played per player per language was 36. We used this number to divide each group of samples into two further groups, those created until the 36th round, and samples produced after that.

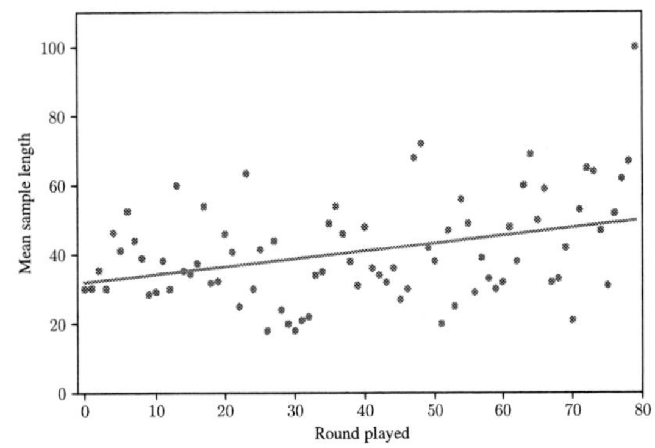

Figure 8: Mean length of beginner Spanish speakers samples across rounds played

Group	Round $\leq$ 36 Mean (SD)	Round > 36 Mean (SD)	p-value
Beginner ES	35.8 (22.59)	48.71 (19.14)	< 0.001
Beginner PT	28.84 (12.22)	35.31 (18.82)	< 0.001
Intermediate ES	36.59 (18.15)	42.54 (16.21)	< 0.001
Intermediate DE	37.3 (23.33)	45.0 (21.59)	< 0.001
Advanced FR	42.68 (21.14)	56.14 (23.89)	< 0.001

Table 4: Sample length by user group until and after 36 rounds

6.3.1 Text length

Once separating the samples further down by language, many groups did not have enough samples for confident results. For example, there were no samples at all produced by English or French beginner speakers after the 36th round and altering the threshold for breaking the groups into before and after to the mean of rounds played for that group did not alter the outcome. For certain groups it was possible to observe significant improvements, as seen on Table 4. A positive trend for Spanish beginner players can be seen on Fig. 8.

6.3.2 Depth of parse-tree

For the second metric, as seen on Table 5, in a breakdown per group level, none presented significant progress, and in a further breakdown per language, only beginner Spanish and advanced French players presented significant improvement.

6.3.3 XLM-r acceptability score

For the third metric, the trend seen in the plot in Fig. 9 shows an overall improvement in average acceptability score. However, as seen on Table 6, beginner and advanced players did not present

Group	Round ≤ 36 Mean (SD)	Round > 36 Mean (SD)	p-value
Beginner All	3.26 (0.89)	3.28 (0.79)	0.64
Intermediate All	3.5 (0.97)	3.58 (0.99)	0.12
Advanced All	3.65 (1.04)	3.64 (1.05)	0.92
Beginner ES	3.26 (0.91)	3.85 (1.0)	< 0.001
Advanced FR	3.35 (0.82)	3.65 (0.95)	< 0.001

Table 5: Depth of parse-tree of sample by user group until and after 36 rounds

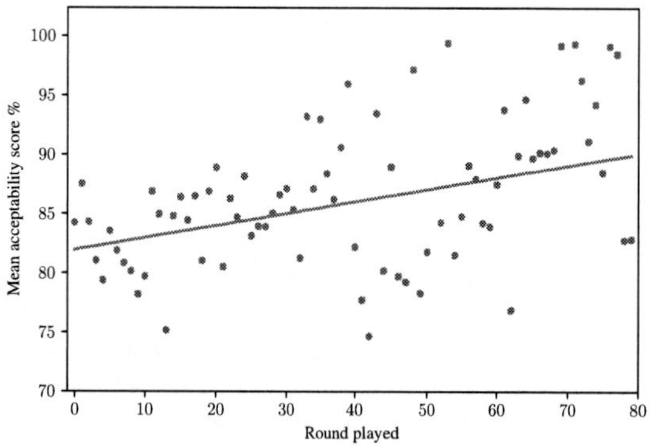

Figure 9: Mean XLM-r acceptability score of non-native speaker samples across rounds played

a significant progress. Meanwhile, intermediary players obtained an average gain of 4.6% in their XLM-r scores on later rounds.

6.4 User Survey

We sent the user questionnaire to all 321 active players, obtaining 61 responses. Many of our questions were formatted as a 1-5 scale where 1-2 is a negative response, 3 is considered neutral, and 4-5 are positive and very positive responses. Based on this, 83.6% respondents indicated that they would recommend Polygloss to a friend learning a language, 77% that it is easy to play, 83% that the game instructions are clear, 75.4% said playing Polygloss is a practical activity for learning, 73.6% that it is useful for learning a language, and 88.6% that it is fun to play. We further divided questions related to usefulness, and the results can be seen on Table 7.

Group	Round ≤ 36 Mean (SD)	Round > 36 Mean (SD)	p-value
Beginner	81.07 (32.41)	82.17(31.73)	0.62
Intermediate	82.53 (31.0)	87.13(26.78)	< 0.01
Advanced	88.09 (25.78)	89.03(25.92)	0.51

Table 6: Mean XLM-r acceptability score across time by user group (%)

In the open fields, the more complimented areas of the game were interacting with other people and the ability to be creative. The most criticized aspects were how difficult the game is for absolute beginners in a language, and the points system, for, despite being intuitive, not giving a sense of progress in the language. Common feature requests were: more ways to track progress, such as streaks, audio matches, and sentence and word examples.

7 Discussion

The division of the mean sample length metric by players' proficiency group suggests that although beginners write shorter texts in comparison with other groups, there is not a significant difference among the other groups. Once breaking the groups down into each language, it is even more difficult to tell. This is an obstacle for comparing progress among them, making it difficult to evaluate learner fit. It is still, however, a positive surprise to see a considerable progress for beginner Spanish and Portuguese and advanced French groups, given they were not part of the intended audience.

The depth of the parse-tree metric behaved differently from our expectations as it presented an odd peak at advanced players, above native speakers. This could mean that this is a bad metric, but one possible explanation for this behavior is that advanced players could be making more effort to write elaborate sentences in order to practice, while native speakers do not bother. Either way, this metric also does not help with evaluating learner fit, especially when breaking the groups down once more for each language. Across time, we understand the lack of significant progress in many groups as a sign that the game is not giving enough incentive to write more elaborately. This is also backed by our user survey, where users point grammar as the aspect with which they thought Polygloss is least helpful.

Indeed, the game does not draw explicit attention to form, which is one of the factors necessary for what Chapelle (2001) calls of *language learning potential*, which further explains these results. If a player writes a sentence containing a grammar mistake, the system does not provide a correction before progressing to the next

	Useful (%)	Neutral (%)	Not useful (%)
Expressing yourself better	62.75	23.53	13.72
Being more confident	55.77	23.08	21.15
Learning real-world sentences	46.15	34.62	19.23
Becoming more proficient	45.76	32.20	22.04
Learning new words	45.26	24.59	31.15
Learning spelling	40.00	40.00	20.00
Learning grammar	13.33	31.67	55.00

Table 7: How do you think Polygloss was useful with...?

round. However, when Chapelle says *language learning potential* in a CALL system is characterized by its difference from being simply an opportunity for language use, we would need to assume that simply using language does not lead to learning gains or we would need to restrict ourselves to a very narrow definition of *use*. In practice, there are many benefits brought by collaborative aspects that arise from language usage (Swain, 2006). Chapelle does include characteristics such as interactional modification and modification of output, which are, in essence, processes that derive from collaborative use. Although this could sound unclear, she does go on to elaborate that the exact meaning of this criterion will evolve as second language acquisition research continues to develop. Given that, it seems that our system does implement then, a partial attention to form, as it allows players to send each other feedback and modify their output. However, like on a real-world interaction, not all mistakes elicit feedback. In Polygloss, only 4.5% of the samples studied received some feedback and, in fact, the user survey also received mentions of it not being enough. One possible explanation for this is that players might be correcting others only when mistakes damage comprehensibility and are an obstacle to the task at hand. Nevertheless, some subgroups like beginner Spanish and Advanced French did show improvements in parse-tree depth across number of rounds played, and intermediate samples showed improvements in the XLM-r scores, which also captures some form.

Results from the XLM-r acceptability score metric showed it to be best suited metric for evaluating learner fit. Given we had no record of it being used in this way before, we are satisfied with how it performed. We understand that grouping languages together also facilitated interpreting the results, given our number of samples. Even if there is not a clear difference in score between advanced and native groups, the difference is clear among the other groups. One factor that could have impacted this is that we did not separate the samples from advanced speakers who were actively learning the language from the ones from players who registered it as a language they spoke, but were using the game to learn another language. For example, one could speak Portuguese at native level, speak advanced English, and be currently learning French, which they also self-evaluated at advanced level. Indeed, only 22% of the players who evaluated their English as advanced had English listed in the languages they wanted to learn, compared with 62% of the advanced French and 68% of the advanced German player groups.

The improvement observed for intermediate level players over number of rounds played is further backed by the user questionnaire, where users indicated that the game is too difficult for beginners. This result validates our intended proposal, since intermediary level speakers were our target audience for this game.

Authenticity, as Chapelle (2001) explains, is the level of correspondence between a language learning task and a task the learner can encounter in the real world, outside the learning environment. The user survey shows good results in this area, as 63.7% of players thought the game helps expressing yourself better and 46.15% thought it helps learning real-world sentences, which are important for authenticity and pragmatics. We observed usage of authenticity when players produced sentences like the one below, where they use the image provided to successfully practice discussing current world events, such as the Covid-19 pandemic, even if the image does not necessarily draw attention to the subject.

The opportunity to make such outputs is allowed by the flexibility to write creatively pro-

"Sie sollten ihre Hände waschen"
(They should wash their hands)

vided by the game's design informed on critical pedagogy. This is also particularly convenient because it does not require frequents updates to the game's content to introduce current discussion topics.

8 Future work

Even though the results are positive and the application was perceived as fun to play, practical and useful by the majority of the players, there are many avenues for future work. The first one is to modify the game to draw more attention to form, add more interaction and collaborative features, encourage players to use the feedback feature more often, and reevaluate the performance on syntactic complexity metrics. Another possible route is to implement word tips and sentence examples and reevaluate the performance of learners on lexical competence metrics. This could be done using the data collected from other players on previous matches and the users own accumulated vocabulary to expand on topics that are interesting to them. Lastly, one other possibility is to allow the matches to be played with audio, and conduct a fluency and phonology based analysis.

9 Conclusion

It is hard to find appropriate learning materials for learners looking to overcome the intermediate plateau. At this stage, it is important to employ a mix of techniques, not abandon active study and produce language using your own words. Our proposed visually-grounded task has proven to be an effective way of doing that. We developed a learning game made available in a practical way as a mobile application, playable at any time of the day, and, given the existence of available partners, sufficiently generic to be playable in any chosen language. Even though more attention could be drawn to form, it draws sufficient attention to meaning, offering creative freedom and opportunity for authenticity. It provides positive impact beyond meaning and form as players feel it helps them express themselves better. Both the quantitative and qualitative results in this study confirm the intended fit of this task for intermediary level language learners and reveal a possible fit for other groups that could be explored in future research. In addition to this primary contribution, a second contribution is the serviceable use of transformers' acceptability score as an evaluation metric. Finally, we would like to join Benson (2013) in his call to have autonomy as an explicit goal in CALL, and highlight the importance of socially informed design for the development of successful language learning applications.

Acknowledgments

This research was supported in part by the DALI project, ERC Grant 695662, in part by the EPSRC CDT in Intelligent Games and Game Intelligence (IGGI), EP/L015846/1.

References

Uju Anya. 2016. *Racialized Identities in Second Language Learning: Speaking Blackness in Brazil*. Routledge Advances in Second Language Studies. Taylor & Francis.

Phil Benson. 2013. *Teaching and Researching: Autonomy in Language Learning*. Applied Linguistics in Action. Taylor & Francis.

Suma Bhat and Su-Youn Yoon. 2014. Automatic assessment of syntactic complexity for spontaneous speech scoring. *Speech Communication*, 67.

Serge Bibauw, Thomas François, and Piet Desmet. 2019. Discussing with a computer to practice a foreign language: research synthesis and conceptual framework of dialogue-based call. *Computer Assisted Language Learning*, pages 1–51.

Robert Blake. 2005. Bimodal CMC: The glue of language learning at a distance. *CALICO Journal*, 22:497–511.

Carol A. Chapelle. 2001. *Computer Applications in Second Language Acquisition*. Cambridge Applied Linguistics. Cambridge University Press.

Council of Europe. 2001. *Common European Framework of Reference for Languages: Learning, Teaching, Assessment*. Cambridge University Press.

Paulo Freire. 1967. *Educação como prática da liberdade*. Série Ecumenismo e humanismo. Paz e Terra.

Paulo Freire. 1972. *Pedagogia do oprimido*. Paz e Terra.

Janosch Haber, Tim Baumgärtner, Ece Takmaz, Lieke Gelderloos, Elia Bruni, and Raquel Fernández. 2019. The photobook dataset: Building common ground through visually-grounded dialogue.

Sylvain Hatier, Arnaud Bey, and Mathieu Loiseau. 2019. Formalism for a language agnostic language learning game and productive grid generation. In *Proceedings of the 8th Workshop on NLP for Computer Assisted Language Learning*, Turku, Finland. LiU Electronic Press.

Alexis Housen, Folkert Kuiken, and Ineke Vedder. 2012. *Complexity, accuracy and fluency: Definitions, measurement and research*, Language Learning amp; Language Teaching, pages 1–20. John Benjamins Publishing Company, Netherlands.

Anisia Katinskaia, Javad Nouri, and Roman Yangarber. 2017. Revita: a system for language learning and supporting endangered languages. In *Proceedings of the joint workshop on NLP for Computer Assisted Language Learning and NLP for Language Acquisition*, pages 27–35, Gothenburg, Sweden. LiU Electronic Press.

Stephen Krashen and Tracy Terrell. 1983. *The Natural Approach: Language Acquisition in the Classroom*. Language Teaching Methodology Series. Pergamon Press.

Guillaume Lample and Alexis Conneau. 2019. Cross-lingual language model pretraining. *Advances in Neural Information Processing Systems (NeurIPS)*.

Jey Lau, Alexander Clark, and Shalom Lappin. 2016. Grammaticality, acceptability, and probability: A probabilistic view of linguistic knowledge. *Cognitive science*, 41.

Hsueh Liu, Karey Lan, and John Jenkins. 2014. Technology-enhanced strategy use for second language vocabulary acquisition. *English Teaching Learning*, 38:105–132.

Huan Liu and Cindy Brantmeier. 2019. "I know english": Self-assessment of foreign language reading and writing abilities among young chinese learners of english. *System*, 80:60–72.

Qing Ma and Peter Kelly. 2006. Computer assisted vocabulary learning: Design and evaluation. *Computer Assisted Language Learning*, 19.

Ernesto Macaro, Zoe Handley, and Catherine Walter. 2012. A systematic review of call in english as a second language: Focus on primary and secondary education. *Language Teaching*, 45.

Tomas Mikolov, Ilya Sutskever, Kai Chen, G.s Corrado, and Jeffrey Dean. 2013. Distributed representations of words and phrases and their compositionality. *Advances in Neural Information Processing Systems*, 26.

Paul Nation and Susan Hunston. 2013. *Learning Vocabulary in Another Language*, 2 edition. Cambridge Applied Linguistics. Cambridge University Press.

Emmanuel Rayner, Pierrette Bouillon, Nikolaos Tsourakis, Johanna Gerlach, Yukie Nakao, and Claudia Baur. 2010. *A Multilingual CALL Game Based on Speech Translation*, Proceedings of LREC. ID: unige:14926.

Frank E. Ritter and Lael J. Schooler. 2001. The learning curve. *International Encyclopedia of the Social Behavioral Sciences*, pages 8602–8605.

Scott Saft, Yumiko Ohara, and Graham Crookes. 2001. Toward a feminist critical pedagogy in a beginning japanese-as-a-foreign-language class. *Japanese Language and Literature*, 35:105–133.

Merrill Swain. 1985. Communicative competence: Some roles of comprehensible input and comprehensible output in its development. *Input in second language acquisition*, 15:165–179.

Merrill Swain. 2006. *Languaging, agency and collaboration in advanced second language proficiency*, pages 95–108. London: Continuum.

Lev S Vygotsky. 1978. Mind in society (m. cole, v. john-steiner, s. scribner, & e. souberman, eds.).

Mark Warschauer. 1996. Computer assisted language learning: an introduction. *Fotos S. (ed.) Multimedia language teaching, Tokyo: Logos International*, pages 3–20.

Alex Warstadt, Amanpreet Singh, and Samuel R. Bowman. 2018. Neural network acceptability judgments. *CoRR*, abs/1805.12471.

Appendices

A User Survey

1. Would you recommend Polygloss to a friend learning a language?
2. Have you been playing Polygloss recently?
3. If you answered "no" to the previous question: Why? Is there anything that would have made you play it more?
4. Do you think Polygloss is easy to play?
5. Do you think the instructions and the tasks you need to do in the game are clear?
6. Do you think playing Polygloss is a practical way to advance your language progress?
7. Do you think Polygloss is useful for learning a language?
8. Do you think Polygloss is fun to play?

9. How do you think polygloss was useful with...? [Learning new words] [Being more communicative] [Being more fluent] [Learning grammar] [Learning spelling] [Learning idiomatic expressions] [Becoming more proficient in the language] [Expressing yourself better] [Being more confident in the language] [Learning sentences you can use in the real world]
10. Is there a feature you would like to see in Polygloss?
11. What would you love to see more often in language learning app?
12. What do you think of Polygloss' interface?
13. How could Polygloss be even better? Do you have any questions about Poygloss?
14. Is there any additional feedback on Polygloss, ideas, anything else you would like to say?

B All samples collected, grouped by language

Language	Beginner	Intermediate	Advanced	Native	Total
English	90	178	621	280	1173
Spanish	304	464	278	108	1168
German	309	454	90	173	1048
French	138	428	436	31	1035
Portuguese	349	152	31	307	852
Greek	259	33	0	129	421
Italian	93	157	54	30	340
Russian	97	41	6	2	148
Japanese	44	19	64	0	128
Dutch	92	18	8	1	120
Swedish	86	10	0	1	97
South Tyrolean	54	0	0	43	97
Polish	21	20	0	19	71
Hungarian	22	37	0	2	61
Indonesian	24	0	0	22	46
Finnish	28	6	0	0	39
Arabic	19	16	0	0	35
Esperanto	26	9	0	0	35
Persian	13	13	0	1	32
Norwegian	17	0	0	1	26
Korean	22	3	0	0	25
Danish	19	0	5	0	24
Mandarin	5	4	4	0	19
Turkish	6	7	0	5	18
Catalan	4	4	4	1	13
Vietnamese	5	0	0	0	9
Croatian	8	0	0	0	8
Javanese	4	0	0	4	8
Hebrew	0	3	0	4	8
Romanian	1	6	0	0	7
Estonian	3	4	0	0	7
Ukrainian	5	0	1	0	6
Slovak	4	0	0	2	6
Afrikaans	2	4	0	0	6
Georgian	5	0	0	0	6
Thai	2	0	0	0	5
Czech	1	0	0	3	4
Bulgarian	4	0	0	0	4
Latin	1	2	0	0	3
Hindi	1	0	0	0	3
Sprok	2	0	1	0	3
Irish	2	0	0	0	2
Scottish Gaelic	1	0	1	0	2
Breton	1	0	0	0	1
Tagalog	1	0	0	0	1
Icelandic	0	0	0	0	1
Serbian	1	0	0	0	1
Total	2195	2092	1604	1169	7060

C Text length performance comparison of proficiency levels broken down by language

Language	Group 1 Mean (SD)	Group 2 Mean (SD)	Welch's unequal variances t-test
English	Beginner 26.31 (11.12)	Intermediary 48.21 (37.54)	t(266) = -7.18, $p < 0.001$
	Intermediary 48.21 (37.54)	Advanced 39.87 (22.41)	t(797) = 2.82, $p < 0.01$
	Advanced 39.87 (22.41)	Native 39.55 (20.51)	t(899) = 0.21, p = 0.8346
Spanish	Beginner 38.14 (22.6)	Intermediary 39.08 (17.63)	t(766) = -0.61, p = 0.5412
	Intermediary 39.08 (17.63)	Advanced 44.38 (25.66)	t(740) = -3.05, $p < 0.01$
	Advanced 44.38 (25.66)	Native 36.31 (23.44)	t(384) = 2.96, $p < 0.01$
German	Beginner 29.49 (12.46)	Intermediary 41.7 (22.7)	t(761) = -9.54, $p < 0.001$
	Intermediary 41.7 (22.7)	Advanced 42.16 (29.16)	t(542) = -0.14, p = 0.8879
	Advanced 42.16 (29.16)	Native 52.97 (32.78)	t(261) = -2.73, $p < 0.01$
French	Beginner 35.62 (26.73)	Intermediary 48.14 (38.95)	t(564) = -4.24, $p < 0.001$
	Intermediary 48.14 (38.95)	Advanced 49.17 (23.52)	t(862) = -0.47, p = 0.6413
	Advanced 49.17 (23.52)	Native 52.32 (36.02)	t(465) = -0.48, p = 0.6339
Portuguese	Beginner 32.14 (16.28)	Intermediary 38.65 (20.99)	t(499) = -3.41, $p < 0.001$
	Intermediary 38.65 (20.99)	Advanced 31.61 (13.44)	t(181) = 2.38, p = 0.0202
	Advanced 31.61 (13.44)	Native 48.12 (35.42)	t(336) = -5.24, $p < 0.001$

Show, Don't Tell: Visualising Finnish Word Formation in a Browser-Based Reading Assistant

Frankie Robertson
University of Jyväskylä
frankie@robertson.name

Abstract

This paper presents the *NiinMikäOli?!* reading assistant for Finnish. The focus is upon the simplified presentation and visualisation of a wide range of word-level linguistic phenomena of the Finnish language in a unified form so as to benefit language learners. The system is available as a browser extension, intended to be used in-context, with authentic texts, in order to encourage free reading in language learners.

1 Introduction

This paper presents an intelligent reading assistant for Finnish. The system, *NiinMikäOli?!* (English: *TheWhatNow?!*), presents word and idiom definitions in-context. The system can be used through a web interface either as a dictionary or by manually entering or copying text into a text field, or ideally, as a browser extension to assist with reading Finnish web pages. When used as a browser extension, *NiinMikäOli?!* presents word definitions in a sidebar.

There is increasing interest in contextualised learning of vocabulary (Godwin-Jones, 2018), and *NiinMikäOli?!* aims to facilitate this in the context of web pages. *NiinMikäOli?!* can be classified as an ATICALL (Authentic Text Intelligent Computer Aided Language Learning) system, defined by Meurers et al. (2010a) as software which produces enhanced input based on real texts.

The focus of this paper is upon *NiinMikäOli?!*'s simplified, unified view of the Finnish language, which uses information visualisation techniques to "show rather than tell" learners about morphological and word formation features. A principle aim is to avoid presentations which tell learners about word-level grammatical features such as technical linguistic language including Latinate names for nominal cases, rather opting to highlight their surface forms. The user interface visualises the connection between surface forms, analytic forms and definitions.

Described first is the construction of the baseline reading assistant system. The system is by and large similar to existing systems such as GLOSSER (Nerbonne et al., 1998) or the reading assistant features of SMILLE (Zilio et al., 2017) or Revita (Katinskaia et al., 2017) – or even very widely used systems such as the WordNet-based alternative translations shown when a single word is selected in Google Translate. Notable as an improvement over some of those systems is *NiinMikäOli?!*'s use of a full scale Word Sense Disambiguation (WSD) system. The rest of this paper describes the motivation behind and implementation of *NiinMikäOli?!*'s visualisations and its exhaustive treatment of complex lexical items such as derived words, compounds and multiword expressions.

2 Baseline system

A combined lexical resource of Finnish was created by combining two sources: FinnWordNet (Lindén and Carlson, 2010) and Wiktionary. The Wiktionary definitions were extracted from publicly available dumps, using a Python script[1] . The Python script parses MediaWiki markup into word senses using `mwparserfromhell`[2].

At least one definition was extracted from 99.8% of a total of 153 196 Wiktionary pages con-

This work is licensed under a Creative Commons Attribution 4.0 International Licence. Licence details: http://creativecommons.org/licenses/by/4.0/.

[1]Available at https://github.com/frankier/wikiparse.

[2]https://github.com/earwig/mwparserfromhell

Frankie Robertson 2020. Show, don't tell: Visualising Finnish word formation in a browser-based reading assistant. *Proceedings of the 9th Workshop on Natural Language Processing for Computer Assisted Language Learning (NLP4CALL 2020)*. Linköping Electronic Conference Proceedings 175: 37–45.

taining *Finnish* as a section heading[3]. Of these, 90 653 are lemmas rather than inflected forms. For comparison, FinnWordNet contains 139 871 headwords, which are mostly lemmas but include occasional idiomatic word forms such as humalassa (literally "in hops").

FinnWordNet is modelled after WordNet, and as such has very fine-grained sense distinctions. This results in potentially overwhelming the learner with too much information. Furthermore, some Wiktionary senses are likely to essentially duplicate FinnWordNet. Thus, similar definitions should be clustered together and only the best definition displayed by default.

The clustering and alignment was created using affinity propagation (Frey and Dueck, 2007). The distances graph is constructed by taking cosine distances between definitions, represented as vectors based on the English text of their definitions according to the English sentence similarity model of Reimers and Gurevych (2019). This model is based on pretrained English BERT models fine-tuned on a semantic similarity task. The pretrained `bert-large-nli-stsb-mean-tokens` model is used. Links between Wiktionary definitions with distinct etymologies are then removed and extra weight is given to Wiktionary definitions so as to encourage them to become exemplars of clusters. The resulting system obtains adjusted rand index scores of 0.48 on a gold standard of WordNet verbs grouped by PropBank sense obtained from Predicate Matrix (de Lacalle et al., 2016), and a score of 0.52 on a manually created clustering of 128 Wiktionary and WordNet noun definitions. The scikit-learn (Pedregosa et al., 2011) implementation of affinity propagation is used.

WSD is performed using UKB (Agirre et al., 2014). Since UKB is a graph based WSD algorithm, it only operates on definitions from FinnWordNet, which are connected by the semantic links from Princeton WordNet. In order to compare WordNet definitions with Wiktionary definitions, the clustering is used. Clusters are then ranked using their best WordNet definition as a representative. Since Wiktionary definitions are usually better for learners, they are pushed to the top of each cluster in the user interface.

[3] In a Wiktionary dump from 6/4/2019.

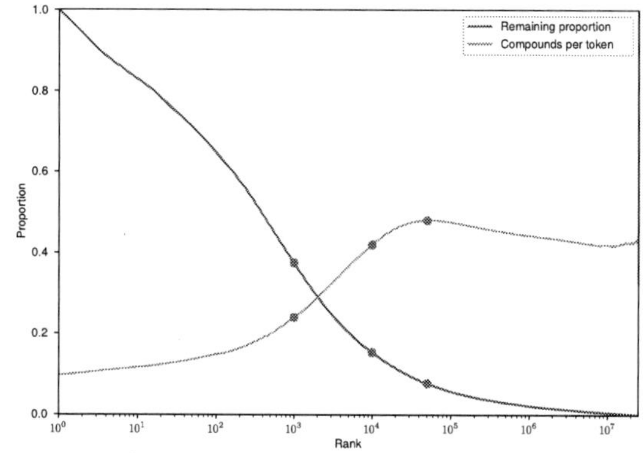

Figure 1: Proportions related to words unknown to a simplified model of a language learner. The x-axis gives the rank of the word that the learner has learned all words up to. Remaining proportion is the proportion of words in running text unknown to the language learner. Compounds per token is the proportion of unknown words which are compounds.

3 Linguistic rationale

Finnish is morphologically rich[4]. Substantives are declined for case and number and verbs are conjugated for person, tense and voice. Finnish word formation is also rich[5]. It includes a number of highly productive derivational morphemes, including many deverbal morphemes which is characteristic of the language. Compounding also plays a major role in Finnish word formation, with many of the compounds being semantically transparent. Finnish also has a number of enclitic particles such as the question forming "-ko/-kö". Finally, it has MWEs (Multi-Word Expressions) such as idioms. In Finnish these may take the form of syntactic frames, treated here as gapped MWEs e.g. "pitää ___-sta", which could occur in a form such as "pidän voileipäkakusta" (English: I like sandwich cake) distinguished from e.g. "pidän voileipäkakun" (English: I keep sandwich cake).

Why bother going to the effort of making a comprehensive treatment of word formation and complex word types? After all, these lexical items occur relatively infrequently in running text and so it may seem like a poor allocation of effort to spend time dealing with them. One assumption here is that these elements become more important after the beginner stage of language learning. If we assume a very simplified model of lexical acquisition where words are learnt in de-

[4] See for example Karlsson (2015).
[5] See for example Hyvärinen (2019).

scending order of frequency, we can analyse properties of words that the language learner does not know and therefore may like to look up. Figure 1 shows two such properties varying as the number of words the learner knows increases: the proportion of all words seen which are unknown, and the proportion of unknown words which are compounds. The data is based on 1.5 billion tokens of analysed Finnish text from the Turku Internet Parsebank (Laippala and Ginter, 2014). Taken as a whole, the corpus is 9.8% compounds. Supposing that an intermediate learner may know somewhere between 1000 and 10 000 words. After learning 1000 words, 24% of unknown words would be compounds, and after 10 000, it would be 42%. Thus quite a large proportion of words unknown to intermediate level learners are compounds. It is assumed that other complex lexical items such as MWEs follow a similar pattern. Here we refer to any item which can be given a definition, including lemmas, individual morphemes and MWEs as *headwords*.

Admitting these items are frequent, the next question becomes, why is simple lemma extraction not sufficient? One argument against performing lemma extraction and simply showing lemmas comes from the noticing hypothesis (Schmidt, 1990) which states that without attention to form (Lightbown and Spada, 2013, pp. 168–175), second language learners in particular are prone to not acquiring fine-grained grammatical knowledge. Following this concept, systems such as those of Meurers et al. (2010b) and Reynolds et al. (2014) were created to automatically enhance input in web pages in order to promote noticing of, for example, parts of speech. *NiinMikäOli?!* follows a similar direction, but instead focusses on morphemes, drawing attention to the connection and overlap between analytic and surface forms, so to promote learning of morphology, as well as attention to the formation of the word itself.

Why analyse words using only normalised segments, rather than — as a lot of reference material for the Finnish language does — using grammatical descriptions, such as Latinate names for case endings. The reason for this is twofold. Firstly, as Bleyhl (2009) notes, treatments of language which are heavy on grammatical analysis and the associated linguistic terminology can be counter-productive in language instruction since they draw attention away from the comprehensible input needed for true language acquisition. This large amount of extra material can lead to reduced confidence from learners. Secondly, due to Finnish's agglutinative morphology, contrasted with a fusional language like Latin, it is simply not necessary to add this extra layer of analytical language, since many Finnish inflectional morphemes occur in the same form or an easily recognisable form at all times, and they can thus be referred to by their normalised form. Consider for example, the Finnish system of locative case endings. These have a fairly good correspondence in terms of function with prepositions in English. Imagine if, when teaching English, every preposition was also given a name to describe it so that we would always refer to "from" as "the elative preposition". It is hard to imagine that a learner would be well served by this extra indirection! This principle is somewhat flexible, however, and the names of the most common case endings — partitive and genitive — are shown on the basis that their usage is more grammatical. They are more often obligated by context rather than used with the intention of conveying extra information. Plural is referred to by-name since it is likely to be familiar.

4 Implementation

The pipeline from running text to analytical segments, described in this section, is shown in Figure 2.

4.1 MWE lexicon & extraction

FinnMWE (Robertson, 2020) is used as a lexicon of MWEs. In order to extract MWEs from running text, for each MWE is indexed by all possible lemmas of a key token. In case the head is known, it is used as the key token, otherwise the rarest token based on wordfreq (Speer et al., 2018) is used. MWEs are then extracted from dependency trees obtained using the Turku neural dependency parsing pipeline (Kanerva et al., 2018). First, all key matches are found simultaneously by looking up all lemmas in the dependency tree. These candidates are filtered by trying to match each remaining token in the MWE against any neighbour, extending the neighbourhood in the process until the whole MWE is matched or it is impossible to proceed. When the MWE key is its head, its parent is excluded from the neighbourhood of potential

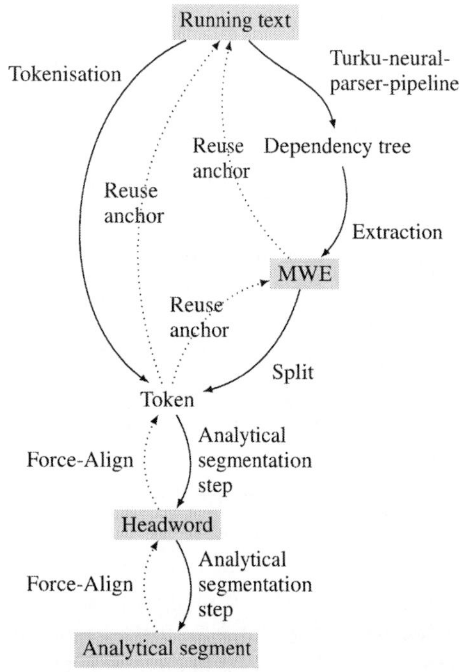

Figure 2: Diagram showing processing pipeline from surface forms to analytical segments. Objects indicated in yellow are linked within the user interface during the hover brushing interaction. Dotted lines indicate how spans corresponding to the in-node are found in the out-node.

matching tokens. MWE tokens without a lemma act as wildcards, and can match multiple tokens, but they must be connected within the dependency tree.[6]

4.2 Analytical segmentation data

The approach to analytical segmentation pursued here is to combine analyses from the Omorfi morphological analyser (Pirinen, 2015) and information from Wiktionary together to produce analytical segmentations. Omorfi produces analyses in its own format, which has some degree of compatibility with tags from the Universal Dependencies (UD) project (Pyysalo et al., 2015). As an example, kakusta may be analysed as `[WORD_ID=kakku] [UPOS=NOUN] [NUM=SG] [CASE=ELA]`. Morphological tags are mapped to analytical morphemes so that e.g. `[CASE=ELA]` is output as -sta, while `WORD_ID` is passed through. The order in which the tags appear is the same order as the surface morphemes appear, meaning our analytical morphemes are in the same order as the surface morphemes.

[6]The MWE extraction code is made available at `https://github.com/frankier/lextract`

Wiktionary contains various template tags which give information about word formation. This data is scraped into a database so that each etymology section can give a derivation for its headword. Template tags are normalised into either inflections, derivations or compounds consisting of normalised segments. For compounds and most derivations, normalised segments are directly available as arguments to the template tag. However, the `agent noun of` template tag, for example, must be manually mapped to "-ja". Finally, the `form of` template tag makes use of grammatical terms such as elative, which are mapped to normalised segments such as "-sta".

4.3 Building segmentation derivations

Complex words may have several levels of compounding or word derivation and inflection. Thus, we may have to make use of several lookups to fully segment a word form. We also want to make sure a completely segmented word form can be associated with all lexical items that make it up. We thus shift our perspective to think of these analyses as rules and the segmenter as a rule engine which applies them to produce derivations subject to constraints. Each rule can match any single segment and produce many segments.

The basic rule engine operates by recursively applying rules. It keeps track of the current front of the derivation tree. At each iteration, each node from the front is considered and one or more steps consisting of applying one or more rules are taken to create child nodes, creating a new front. There may be multiple rules which can match a segment. In this case, all combinations of rules matching each matchable segment are applied. When either there are no more rules which match, or there is a match which does not expand any segments, the node is marked as terminal.

A simple approach would be to allow all rules to apply at once. However, Omorfi analyses do not work very well as rules as-is in our case, for example for voileipäkakusta Omorfi produces three different analyses of different levels of decompounding of voileipäkakku. If we were to apply each of these analyses as rules we would end up with 3 final segmentations. However, for our purposes, they should all be subsumed under the same derivation. Therefore we take the following approach:

1. First, apply Wiktionary based rules recursively.
2. Fetch all Omorfi rules resulting from looking up the whole word form
3. While there are Omorfi rules left:
    (a) Remove any Omorfi rules already subsumed by the current derivation.
    (b) If any rules remain, apply the one producing the least new segments and discard.
    (c) Apply Wiktionary based rules recursively.
4. Apply any retrofitting rules, which exist to deal with occasional cases of fusional Finnish morphology.

For example voileipäkakusta (English: out of/from sandwich cake) would produce the following derivation:

Example 1: voileipäkakusta

→ voileipäkakku sta	*Omorfi: voileipäkakusta*
→ voileipä kakku sta	*Wiktionary: voileipäkakakku*
→ voi leipä kakku sta	*Wiktionary: voileipä*

While voimakkaammin (English: more powerfully) would produce the following:

Example 2: voimakkaammin

→ voimakkaasti mpi	*Wiktionary: voimakkaammin*
→ voimakas sti mpi	*Wiktionary: voimakkaasti*
→ voima kas sti mpi	*Wiktionary: voimakas*
→ voida ma kas sti mpi	*Wiktionary: voima*

In this case a retrofitting rule mmin → sti mpi[7] can be applied:

Example 3: voimakas sti mpi

← voimakas mmin	*Retrofit: mmin*
← voimakkaammin	*Connect to parent*

4.4 Constraints upon rules

Applied as-is, this scheme will produce impossible segmentations. However, if we consider the POS (Part-Of-Speech) of each segment, we can place constraints to ameliorate this.

We use a simple set of POS tags based on WordNet: Verb, Noun, Adverb, Adjective & Unknown. The UD POS tags used by Omorfi and the Wiktionary POS headings are mapped into this common scheme. The mapping is lossy, for example, UD adpositions are mapped onto the Adverb POS. All closed classes, interjections and affixes are mapped to Unknown. Note that constituent words of Finnish compounds can be inflected words, and so here inflected forms are treated as having the POS of their lemma.

[7] "-sti" is adverb forming morpheme like "-ly", while "-mpi" is a comparative forming morpheme like "-er".

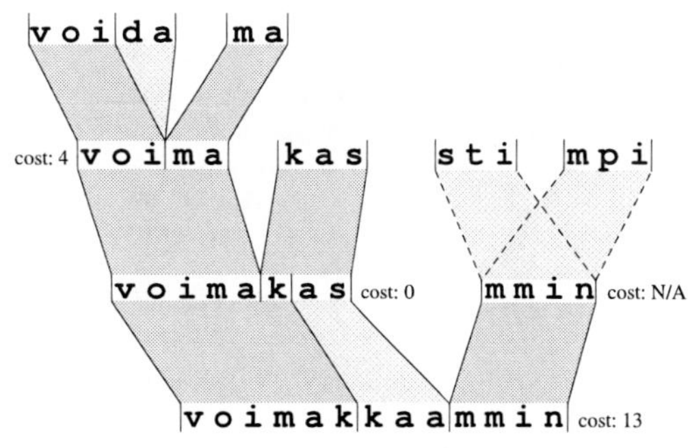

Figure 3: Alignment within derivation tree of voimakkaammin. Dark yellow portions denote surface spans, while each of the whole yellow portions including dark and light denote the whole logical span. The cost of each alignment according to Force-Align is shown next to the parent segment. The dashed lines indicate the alignment is not produced by Force-Align but instead obtained from the underlying rule. In this case: the synthetic rule -mmin → -sti -mpi.

The permissible compound POS patterns can then be produced by a list of production rules, obtained by studying Hyvärinen (2019):

Verb → Noun Verb (e.g., koe+lentää)
Verb → Adverb Verb (e.g., edes+auttaa)
Noun → Noun Noun (e.g., voi+leipä)
Noun → Adjective Noun (e.g., puna+viini)
Adjective → Adjective Adjective (e.g., hyvän+näköinen)

We start by treating the whole token as having Unknown POS, meaning we can match any POS. At any time a segment is constrained to having one of a set of POS tags. For compounds of more than two parts, we can obtain the possible POS patterns by expanding the production rules given above.

Referring back to Example 1, a Wiktionary rule allows the analysis of voi (Verb) as voida (3rd pers.), however voileipäkakku is known to be a Noun, meaning according to the above rules, voi must be either a Noun or an Adjective, meaning this rule cannot be applied.

4.5 Obtaining alignments from derivations

In order to find correspondences between individual characters in analytical segments, surface forms and headwords, we apply the Force-Align procedure at each step of the analytical segmentation derivation. Each child segment is given a span into the parent segment. These are ordered and non-overlapping. Matches are performed af-

```
Function FORCE-ALIGN(parent string p, array of
  child strings c_1 ... c_n )
  returns alignment a
    Create a bounded priority queue pq with the
      lowest cost partial solution at its front
    Add an empty partial solution into pq
    while the head of pq is not complete do
        Pop partial solution j from front of pq
        /* Make a match                      */
        if j's cursor into c has not reached end and
          j's cursor into p has not reached end and
          p_(j's cursor into p) = c_(j's cursor into c)
        then
            Add copy of j into pq with its cursors
              into p and c incremented
        end
        /* Skip a parent character           */
        if j's cursor into p is not at beginning or
          end then
            Add copy of j into pq with its cursor
              into p and its parent characters
              skipped incremented
        end
        /* Skip the rest of the
           current child segment             */
        if j's cursor into p is not at beginning and
          j's cursor into c has not reached end then
            Add copy of j into pq with its cursor
              into c and its child characters
              skipped incremented
        end
    end
    a := alignment formed by solution at front of pq
end
```

Algorithm 1: The Force-Align procedure to find an alignment between a parent string and its segmented children strings.

ter normalisation. All strings are lowercased and the front vowels ä, ö and y are mapped to the respective back vowels a, o and u. We aim to minimise a cost defined as the sum of the square of the number of parent characters skipped and square of the number of child characters skipped. An example showing the type of alignments produced by Force-Align applied to the derivation of voimakkaammin is shown in Figure 3.

Force-Align is implemented as a dynamic programming style procedure, given as pseudocode in Algorithm 1. At each step, Force-Align keeps track of candidate solutions in a priority queue, with the lowest cost partial solution always being at the front. The priority queue has bounded length to bound the running time — making the procedure a form of beam search. Whenever a partial candidate solution is taken from the front of the queue, up to three new partial solutions are created and added back to the priority queue: making a single character match; skipping a single character from the parent string; and skipping the rest of the characters in the current child segment. The procedure ends when there is a complete solution at the front of the queue. Each child segment's full span covers the characters from the beginning of its first character match to just before the first character match of the next child segment, or until the end of the parent segment in the case of the last child segment.

A span of a segment onto any ancestor segment can be found by following a simple rule at each step: shift the whole span rightwards by far enough to fit any new segments to the left, and extend the right edge to the end of the child span onto the parent segment while the current child segment is the rightmost. As an example, consider Figure 3 and the analytical morpheme -kas. It begins on the right edge. We consider its alignment onto voimakas and find we must shift its left edge by five characters to make space for voima. We replace its right edge with that of its parent, which does not change the span. -kas is still on the right edge of voimakas when we consider the alignment of voimakas and voimakkaammin. At this step, we do not have to shift the left edge since there are no new segments to the left. The right edge is replaced with the right edge of the alignment of voimakas onto voimakkaammin, shifting it right by one character. The final span contains the characters 'kkaa' — which is the allomorph corresponding to 'kas', as required.

When the user hovers over a segment of a segmentation in the user interface, the corresponding surface form of the same segment should highlight. The highlighting consists of a strong highlight for that part of the surface form which has overlapping text with the analytic form, and a weak highlight for that part which is grammatically part of the same morpheme but does not literally match. The strong highlight is found by finding the longest match between the child segment and its span within the parent segment, while the weak highlight is made from any part of the span which is left over.

Special consideration is given to wildcards, such as ___-sta. In this case, matching is performed right to left, and the wildcard is weakly matched against that which remains after all other analytic segments are aligned.

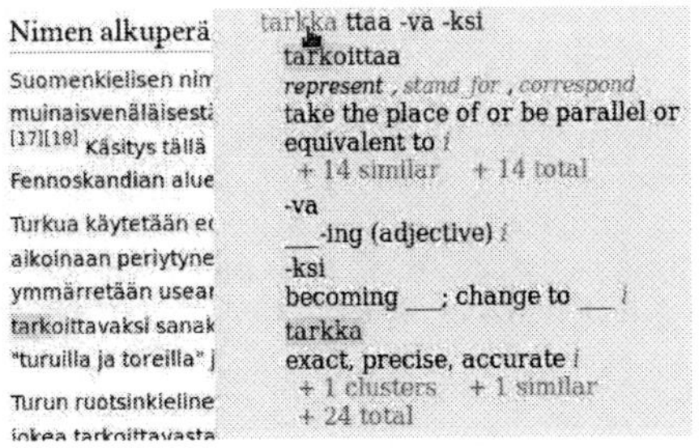

Figure 4: A screenshot showing the Finnish Wikipedia page *Turku* being read using the browser extension.

5 Visualising Finnish word formation

A screenshot of the user interface is shown in Figure 4. Definitions are grouped by normalised segmentation. Within each normalised segmentation there are defined headwords, each corresponding to one or more of the normalised segments. They are ordered in decreasing order of coverage of the normalised segmentation, meaning those definitions which define the meaning of the surface form most closely appear closest to the top. Within each defined headword appears one or more clusters of definitions, each with an exemplar.

To bring attention back to surface forms from the normalised forms, the interface highlights the surface forms as the learner hovers over the segmented forms, as shown in Figure 5. The interaction recalls a one dimensional "hover scrub" action. Initially, the whole word or phrase is lightly highlighted. As the learner scrubs over analytic morphemes, the corresponding spans in the surface form are highlighted.

To show the connection between the normalised segmentation and its definitions, parts of the defined headwords are highlighted when normalised segments are hovered over, as shown in Figures 4 & 5. The whole interaction serves to link the different views of surface form, analytical form and headwords.[8]

6 Conclusions and Future Work

This paper presented *NiinMikäOli?!* The system streamlines the experience of using reference material by presenting it in-context, emphasising the most important parts and presenting simplified grammatical analyses which do not rely upon technical linguistic jargon, following the principle of "show, don't tell".

[8]The NiinMikäOli?! browser extension and website are available at `https://niinmikaoli.fi/`, while the analytical segmentation code is available at `https://github.com/frankier/asafi`.

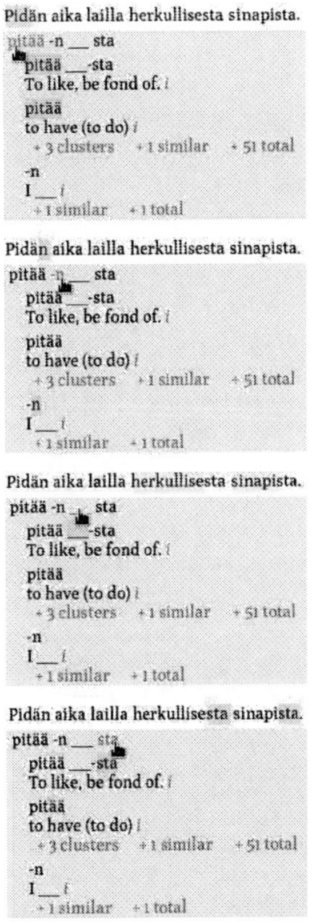

Figure 5: A composite screenshot showing different stages of the interaction resulting when a user brushes over segments in the text analyser.

Clearly, the question of whether systems such as *NiinMikäOli?!* truly help language learners is a pertinent one. Quantitative user evaluation to validate existing features and point to new ones is thus an important piece of future work.

NiinMikäOli?! gives definitions in English. Adding common L1 languages of Finnish learners such as Swedish, Russian or Arabic, as well as Finnish itself could be a useful addition.

The current analytical segmenter is rule based, and thus cannot handle out of vocabulary words. A machine learning approach such as that of Kann et al. (2016) could be combined with the data developed here to address this.

A future direction for all reading assistants is better prediction of language learner needs, which would lead to a system which knows beforehand which types of reading assistance would be best to offer either by explicitly requesting information from the learner, or implicitly using information from previous interactions with the software.

References

Eneko Agirre, Oier Lopez de Lacalle, and Aitor Soroa. 2014. Random walks for knowledge-based word sense disambiguation. *Computational Linguistics*, 40(1):57–84.

Werner Bleyhl. 2009. The hidden paradox of foreign language instruction. or: Which are the real foreign language learning processes. *Input Matters in SLA. Clevedon: Multilingual Matters*, pages 137–55.

Brendan J. Frey and Delbert Dueck. 2007. Clustering by passing messages between data points. *Science*, 315(5814):972–976.

Robert Godwin-Jones. 2018. Contextualized vocabulary learning. *Language Learning & Technology*, 22(3):1–19.

Irma Hyvärinen. 2019. *Compounds and multi-word expressions in Finnish: Compounds and Multi-Word Expressions*, pages 307–336. De Gruyter.

Jenna Kanerva, Filip Ginter, Niko Miekka, Akseli Leino, and Tapio Salakoski. 2018. Turku neural parser pipeline: An end-to-end system for the conll 2018 shared task. In *Proceedings of the CoNLL 2018 Shared Task: Multilingual Parsing from Raw Text to Universal Dependencies*, pages 133–142. Association for Computational Linguistics.

Katharina Kann, Ryan Cotterell, and Hinrich Schütze. 2016. Neural morphological analysis: Encoding-decoding canonical segments. In *Proceedings of the 2016 Conference on Empirical Methods in Natural Language Processing*, pages 961–967, Austin, Texas. Association for Computational Linguistics.

Fred Karlsson. 2015. *Finnish: an essential grammar*. Routledge.

Anisia Katinskaia, Javad Nouri, and Roman Yangarber. 2017. Revita: a system for language learning and supporting endangered languages. In *Proceedings of the joint workshop on NLP for Computer Assisted Language Learning and NLP for Language Acquisition*, pages 27–35, Gothenburg, Sweden. LiU Electronic Press.

Maddalen Lopez de Lacalle, Egoitz Laparra, Itziar Aldabe, and German Rigau. 2016. A multilingual predicate matrix. In *Proceedings of the Tenth International Conference on Language Resources and Evaluation (LREC'16)*, pages 2662–2668, Portorož, Slovenia. European Language Resources Association (ELRA).

Veronika Laippala and Filip Ginter. 2014. Syntactic n-gram collection from a large-scale corpus of internet finnish. In *Human Language Technologies-The Baltic Perspective: Proceedings of the Sixth International Conference Baltic HLT*, volume 268, page 184.

P. M. Lightbown and N. Spada. 2013. *How languages are learned*, 3rd ed edition. Oxford handbooks for language teachers. Oxford University Press.

Krister Lindén and Lauri Carlson. 2010. Finnwordnet–finnish wordnet by translation. *LexicoNordica–Nordic Journal of Lexicography*, 17:119–140.

Detmar Meurers, Ramon Ziai, Luiz Amaral, Adriane Boyd, Aleksandar Dimitrov, Vanessa Metcalf, and Niels Ott. 2010a. Enhancing authentic web pages for language learners. In *Proceedings of the NAACL HLT 2010 Fifth Workshop on Innovative Use of NLP for Building Educational Applications*, pages 10–18. Association for Computational Linguistics.

Detmar Meurers, Ramon Ziai, Luiz Amaral, Adriane Boyd, Aleksandar Dimitrov, Vanessa Metcalf, and Niels Ott. 2010b. Enhancing authentic web pages for language learners. In *Proceedings of the NAACL HLT 2010 Fifth Workshop on Innovative Use of NLP for Building Educational Applications*, pages 10–18. Association for Computational Linguistics.

J. Nerbonne, D. Dokter, and P. Smit. 1998. Morphological processing and computer-assisted language learning. *Computer Assisted Language Learning*, 11(5):543–559.

Fabian Pedregosa, Gaël Varoquaux, Alexandre Gramfort, Vincent Michel, Bertrand Thirion, Olivier Grisel, Mathieu Blondel, Peter Prettenhofer, Ron Weiss, Vincent Dubourg, et al. 2011. Scikit-learn: Machine learning in python. *Journal of machine learning research*, 12(Oct):2825–2830.

Tommi A Pirinen. 2015. Development and use of computational morphology of finnish in the open source and open science era: Notes on experiences with omorfi development. *SKY Journal of Linguistics*, 28:381–393.

Sampo Pyysalo, Jenna Kanerva, Anna Missilä, Veronika Laippala, and Filip Ginter. 2015. Universal dependencies for Finnish. In *Proceedings of the 20th Nordic Conference of Computational Linguistics (NODALIDA 2015)*, pages 163–172, Vilnius, Lithuania. Linköping University Electronic Press, Sweden.

Nils Reimers and Iryna Gurevych. 2019. Sentence-BERT: Sentence embeddings using Siamese BERT-networks. In *Proceedings of the 2019 Conference on Empirical Methods in Natural Language Processing and the 9th International Joint Conference on Natural Language Processing (EMNLP-IJCNLP)*, pages 3982–3992, Hong Kong, China. Association for Computational Linguistics.

Robert Reynolds, Eduard Schaf, and Detmar Meurers. 2014. A VIEW of Russian: Visual input enhancement and adaptive feedback. In *Proceedings of the third workshop on NLP for computer-assisted language learning*, pages 98–112, Uppsala, Sweden. LiU Electronic Press.

Frankie Robertson. 2020. Filling the ___-s in finnish mwe lexicons. In *Joint Workshop on Multiword Expressions and Electronic Lexicons (MWE-LEX 2020)*, Online. Association for Computational Linguistics.

Richard W. Schmidt. 1990. The Role of Consciousness in Second Language Learning. *Applied Linguistics*, 11(2):129–158.

Robyn Speer, Joshua Chin, Andrew Lin, Sara Jewett, and Lance Nathan. 2018. Luminosoinsight/wordfreq: v2.2.

Leonardo Zilio, Rodrigo Wilkens, and Cédrick Fairon. 2017. Using NLP for enhancing second language acquisition. In *Proceedings of the International Conference Recent Advances in Natural Language Processing, RANLP 2017*, pages 839–846, Varna, Bulgaria. INCOMA Ltd.

Association for Computational Linguistics
209 N. Eighth Street
Stroudsburg, Pennsylvania 18360

ISBN 978-1-7138-2834-1

CURRAN ASSOCIATES INC.
proceedings.com